DAVY CROCKETT

INTERNATIONAL FOLKLORE

Advisory Editor
Richard M. Dorson

Editorial Board
Issachar Ben Ami
Vilmos Voigt

*See last pages of this volume
for a complete list of titles*

Davy Crockett

AMERICAN COMIC LEGEND

Selected and edited by
Richard M[ercer] Dorson

ARNO PRESS

A New York Times Company

New York / 1977

Editorial Supervision: LUCILLE MAIORCA

———◆———

Reprint Edition 1977 by Arno Press Inc.

INTERNATIONAL FOLKLORE
ISBN for complete set: 0-405-10077-9
See last pages of this volume for titles.

Manufactured in the United States of America

———◆———

Library of Congress Cataloging in Publication Data

Dorson, Richard Mercer, 1916-   ed.
    Davy Crockett, American comic legend.

    (International folklore)
    Reprint of the 1939 ed. printed at the Spiral Press
for Rockland Editions, New York.
    Includes bibliographical references.
    1. Crockett, David, 1786-1836--Legends. 2. Folk-
lore--United States. 3. American wit and humor.
I. Title. II. Series.
GR105.37.D3D67 1977b   398.2'2'0973   77-70590
ISBN 0-405-10091-4

Davy Crockett

AMERICAN COMIC LEGEND

Selected and edited by Richard M. Dorson. With

a foreword by Howard Mumford Jones. Printed at

the Spiral Press for Rockland Editions, New York

EDITOR'S NOTE

No more genuine expression of the epic frontier exists than in these quaint little almanacs, with their grotesque woodcuts and eye-straining print. They were published from 1835 to 1856, first in Nashville, then in New York and Boston as their fame spread; Philadelphia, Albany, Baltimore and Louisville imprints attest their popularity. In form similar to the numerous comic almanacs of the day, their appearance belies their content, for they are a virtually untapped magic source of frontier lore in all its varied aspects — realistic stories of Indian fighting and pioneer heroes; fantastic adventures of legendary characters; descriptions of wild life and nature sketches; anecdotes of the far-flung frontier from Kentucky to California. The uniquely American figure that emerged from *The Sketches and Eccentricities of Col. David Crockett* in 1833 and the *Narrative of the Life of David Crockett* in 1834 grows to bizarre proportions in the series of Crockett Almanacs; from the cumulative myth is shaped the outlines of America's first superman, grinning with the silent humor of the day.

CONTENTS

vi

DAVY IN LIGHTER MOMENTS

A REGULAR ROW IN THE BACKWOODS

FOREWORD

For most contemporary Americans the picturesque West survives mainly as rodeos, dude ranches, the horse opera of the movies and an occasional visit to the circus, provided the circus still retains the tradition of Pawnee Bill, the hard-riding scout who rescues the stagecoach from Indians whooping it up for the edification of the reserved seat section and the common people. Its literary expression is, alas! reduced to the nostalgic fiction of Will James on one plane, of Zane Grey on another, and of the pulp-paper thrillers (admirable as they are) on yet a third. We also remember Calamity Jane and Wild Bill Hickok.

But if the plain people still know about the West, if an occasional European child yet hopes to find cowboys in Buffalo, New York, the old middle western frontier has receded so deep into the past as to have become the special property of the literary only. Pursuit of information about Dan'el Boone or Simon Kenton has become a job for the historically minded; the tall tale of the southwest is the special pride of a little group of seekers after the roots of American humor; and original editions of books in which humorists sought to convulse the Jacksonian era and its successors are now the pride of bibliophiles and the envy of collectors. When a popular tradition is once embalmed in the sales catalogues of book auctions, it is dead; and not even the excellent zeal of learned fellows like Franklin J. Meine and Bernard DeVoto can revive it as a living thing. I regret to report that though Harvard undergraduates can instantly sing "There's A Long, Long Trail A-Winding," they have to be taught the words and music of "Jesse James." Even Leatherstocking has become the possession of the schoolma'ams who never saw a frontier rifle.

If, seventy-five years ago, anyone had suggested that Davy Crockett was somebody you had to look up in a book, he would have been looked upon as insane and un-American. Davy Crockett was a living reality like George Washington, Napoleon, and Satan. He was an immortal part of the national mythology, secure of a place in the American pantheon. Who

xi

was there to dislodge him? Mike Fink? Alone and unaided, excellent woman that she was, Mrs. Crockett (whose full name, "Sally Ann Thunder Ann Whirlwind Crockett," has the true Homeric splendor) thrashed Fink till he fainted away; and if the distaff side possessed such prowess, who could defeat her greater husband, reared as he was on whiskey out of a bladder, rattlesnakes' eggs, bear's meat, and mustard by the pint? At the age of six he slaughtered four wolves. In his manhood he bit a rattlesnake to death. On an especially cold morning he casually beat enough "hot ile" out of a bear to thaw the earth's "axes" so that the sun could rise and shine. Nothing daunted the immortal Dave:

The snakes spit blue and red lightnin' at me, the big bears growled all sorts o' low thunder, the wolves howled all sorts o' north-east hurrycanes, while the panthers an' Mexican tigers screamed loud enough to set an edge on the teeth of a mill-saw.

But Crockett simply "licked the whole den of varmints so that they came and licked my hands in the most prostrate position —and they have formed my family circle ever since." Hercules was nothing to this.

On the other hand, Davy had the heart of gold which Americans associate with a shagbark exterior. In the great shooting-match between Mike Fink and Crockett, when Fink shot half her comb out of his wife's head, the tender hero admitted defeat: "Davy Crockett's hand would be sure to shake, if his iron war pointed within a hundred mile of a shemale, and I give up beat, Mike." It is true that his trip to Texas and Mexico "sort o' petrified an' soured my cream of human kindness," but on the whole, philanthropy was characteristic of the family. Sister Comfort Crockett, it is recorded, wore out "seven of her nine constitutions" in saving travellers from freezing, famine, wolves and vultures.

Wasteful of our literary inheritance as we have been of our natural resources, we have forgotten Crockett and what he stood for. But if he has passed from the memory of the populace, there is no reason why oblivion should wholly overcome him. If we cannot have him orally around a campfire, let us

at least have him typographically in a book. Through these
excerpts from the Crockett Almanacs, Mr. Dorson reminds us
of the gods we have destroyed. Even in the pale simulacrum
of reprinted material we catch some hint of the exhaustless
energy we once accepted as a matter of course. Mr. Dorson
does well to remind us of our great tradition. A United States
with Crockett for president, Paul Bunyan for secretary of state,
Tony Beaver in the treasury, and Mike Fink at the head of
the war department would not long suffer a depression or de-
bate its foreign policy. They were ringtailed roarers. When
they shouted louder than the myrmidons of Achilles, the
British lion trembled, the Gallic eagle withdrew, and the Spanish dons turned white and were abashed.

The Crockett of the almanacs is, of course, not the Crockett
of the autobiography, and neither is quite the Crockett of
history. It is instructive to watch the literary transformation
which Crockett undergoes. In his final, or epic, incarnation he
is the creation of wild, poetic energy. The impression of law-
less lyricism is, I think, the most lasting impression I carry
away from this material. I do not refer to physical exuberance
only, or to the mere extravagance of linguistic humor, but to
the invention of words and phrases of almost lyric charm. The
metaphoric language of the almanacs, when it is at its best, has
all the freshness of dawn. Crockett, going into the woods for
an airing, tells us he forgot to take his thunderbolt along. A
panther approached him. The beast growled; Crockett "grated
thunder with his teeth." Beast and man confront each other,
"our eyes shootin' horrid, an' blazin' white fire like dead lightnin' afore a gust breaks out." Eyes have blazed fire before, but
the comparison of "dead lightnin' afore a gust breaks out" is
the work of a poet. And after the inevitable battle the panther,
tamed, goes home with Crockett, lights the fire on a dark night
with flashes from his eyes, brushes the hearth every morning
with his tail, and rakes the garden with his claws. To parallel
these extraordinary inventions we have to hunt in other literatures — for example, the wonderful conceptions which are found
in Welsh and Irish tales. The language of mythology is, by

convention, more beautifully molded, but the lyric exuberance is much the same.

Everyone will notice the broad humor, the slap-stick comedy, the verbal burlesque, the outrages on logic and commonsense in this material. But there is also in it an amazing amount of poetically imaginative invention. Put aside the grotesqueness and the spelling in the description of Crockett's sister, for example, and the imagery is the work of a poet, Titanic in its dimensions:

And when she sung a psalm, you'd a thought all the trees in creation war organ pipes, and a harrycane war blowin' the bellows.

Or take even a minor figure like the bully of Salt River, who "sunned himself in a thunder storm," "went to meeting on two horses," and called himself "the great oak that grows half its length underground, and turns up its roots unexpected." This is like something in the *Mabinogion.* One may tire of the conscious striving to be comic, but the lyric invention, when it appears, is always fresh and wonderful.

We do not know who composed the Crockett almanacs. Whoever they were, they were skillful literary technicians. For the populace they supplied the spelling, the invention of comic words, the creation of outrageous phrases. Strip off these outward habiliments of the style, however, and you will find a wonderfully flexible English prose. The cadences fall in the right places, the antitheses are surely placed, the sentences are swift and adroit. If there was a single originator, he taught his imitators well.

But like a long-winded chairman I delay the meeting. Mr. Dorson's introduction explains the nature of these materials and discusses their significance. To what he there says I have only to add that his transcripts of the Crockett almanacs have been carefully made; and that in republishing this material, he is performing a real service for the understanding of the American mind.

HOWARD MUMFORD JONES

FRONTIER HUMOR
AND LEGEND

The American frontier gave birth to a humorous literature and a comic mythology. In oral tale and written anecdote were preserved the grotesque colors thrown on the backwoods scene in the fantasies of the frontiersman; America's nearest approach to the dignity of a legendary past is in this brawling, earthy, boldly-tinted literature, whose surface crudeness still conceals its subtle-witted undertones.

Southern and Southwestern humor, so called, is identified by its locale. It is the local color of frontier life that raises it above the level of dinginess and drabness of much unpalatable American humor — which is why Mark Twain is appetizing today where Artemus Ward, Petroleum V. Nasby, Bill Nye and forgotten scores of their lesser contemporaries are indigestible.

There are a number of conventions that readily mark this frontier humor, and give it its most agreeable features. The most obvious ones are the frontier boast, backwoods invective and imagery, racy dialect, ugly people, earthiness. The language itself is less a convention than an inevitable premise; certainly the mouth-twisting dialect and vernacularisms of the southern yarn-spinners have a picturesqueness entirely lacking in the deliberate misspellings of the later professional funny men.

The frontier boast is probably the best known device of the southern humorists. It brings to mind the characteristic picture of the "gamecock of the wilderness" jumping up in the air, cracking his heels, and exclaiming, "I kills bar, whips panters in a fair fight; I walks the water, out-bellers the thunder, and when I gets hot, the Mississippi hides itself."[1] Exuberance mounted as the gamecock was carried away by his own eloquence.

"I am a raal ringtailed roarer of a jaw breaker, from the thunder and lightning country, down east. I make my breakfast on stewed Yankee and pork steak, and by way of digestion, rinse them down with spike nails and epsom salts; I take dinner of roast goose, stuff'd with wild cats and onions; I sup on nothing but wind; I can sneeze the coat off Colonel Crockett's back, from down east to Tennessee; I can lick my weight and the Colonel's in wild cats or racoons; I can grin steamboat machinery out of place, and snort Major Jack Downing from Washington to his Uncle Jonathan's barn yard. I am just what you may call a real snorter and gall burster. I can out-eat, out-drink, out-work, out-grin, out-snort, out-run, out-lift, out-sneeze, out-sleep, out-lie any thing in the shape of a man or beast, from Maine to Louisiana."[2]

And so on, with endless variations. The unabashed hunter was alternately a snapping turtle, a half-horse half-alligator, the yaller blossom of the forest, a tornado. He could take a steamboat on his back, stand three streaks of lightning without dodging, and put a rifle ball through the moon. And as a matter of course he could always whip his weight in wildcats.

Loquacity and exaggeration feature the monologue, taciturnity and evasion the dialogue of the frontiersman, who sedulously avoided the truth in either circumstance. The inane dialogue that recurred in backwoods conversation is a commonplace in both Yankee and Southwestern humor.

"... Good morning, mister. I don't exactly recall your name, now," said the landlord as I alighted.

"It's of no consequence," said I.

"I'm pretty sure I've seen you somewhere."

"Very likely you may, I've been there frequently."

"I was sure 'twas so; but strange I should forget your name," says he.

"It is indeed somewhat strange that you should forget what you never knew," says I ...[3]

Such byplay would continue until the curious one realized the futility of questioning the canny backwoodsman.

But when the discussion turned acrid, the backwoodsman uncovered a surprising fluency of invective for such a close-lipped fellow. In his wrath he rose to almost poetic heights of malediction, pouring forth his words of opprobrium with a resourcefulness and ingenuity quite incommensurate with his subsequent actions.

"... you monstracious grate hypocrit, you oncivil, lying, pestiliferous vagrandizin scorpion ..."[4]

"He was the durndest, rantankerous hoss-fly that ever clum er tree!"[5]

"... you no-souled, shad-bellied, squash-headed, old night-owl you! — you hay-hookin', corn-cribbin', fodder-fudgin', cent-shavin', whitlin'-of-nuthin' you!"[6]

"... the durnd infunel, hiperkritical, pot-bellied, scaley-hided, whisky-wastin, stinkin ole groun'-hog."[7]

It was not only the promptings of malice that inspired such a display of verbal imagery. Creatures of the woods scurried through the talk of frontier folk; colors from nature dyed their words with extravagant hues. The vivid simile, the picturesque phrase, the unexpected twists of expression sprout luxuriantly on frontier soil.

"... es black es a crow's wing et midnite, ur a nigger hanlin charcoal when he's hed no breakfus ..." (or) "... es hit wud be tu a bline flea on a black cat's fur, an' hit onder forty bushil of wet charcoal dust."[8]

"... fame is like a shaved pig with a greased tail, and it is only after it has slipped through the hands of some thousands, that some fellow, by mere chance, holds on to it!"[9]

(Crockett's recipe for cooking bear-steaks.) "Salt 'em in a hail storm, pepper 'em with buckshot, and then broil 'em with a flash o' lightnin'."[10]

"She was weak in two of her legs, but 'tother two — oh my stars and possum dogs! they make a man swaller tobacker jist to look at 'em, and feel sorter like a June bug was crawlin up his trousers and the waistband too tite for it to git out."[11]

"... an' yu'll mon'sous soon see a bal'-headed man hot enuf tu fry spit."[12]

"She used to brag that she war a streak of litenin set up edgeways and buttered with quicksilver."[13]

"I sot these yere laigs a-gwine onder three hunder' pound presure of pure scare. Long es they is, they went apast each uther as fas' as the spokes of two spinnin wheels a runnin contrary ways."[14]

"Now and then you may see the cabin of a squatter, stuck to the side of a hill, like a discharged tobacco-quid against a wall."[15]

Words as well as phrases acquired the homespun touch of the backwoods. But whereas his descriptive expressions served to clarify his meaning, the backwoodsman's outlandish word-concoctions seemed the rather to obscure it effectively. Gawky adjectives — ramstugenous, daggerified, indignitorious, gully-whumping, slantendickler, poxtakedest; embarrassed verbs — discomboberate, codgertate, explunctificate, rumsquattle, absquatulate; and shamefaced nouns — homogification, sorritude, circumbustifikashun, flutterbation, peedoddles, solumkolly, are sprinkled through almost every page of frontier humor.[16]

An eccentricity even more conspicuous than the use of ugly words is the description of ugly people. Pride in ugliness, or in the ability to depict ugliness, was a favorite tradition of the frontier; the more misshapen, cadaverous, leperlike, or generally hideous the individual under discussion, the more accomplished the raconteur. No macabre detail was overlooked in presenting these monsters. For instance:

"His eyes were like a pair of preserved beans; nature had made an excavation in the centre of his nose; his lips were like a large plumb that became cracked in the centre from being overripe; there was a hollow in his chin as if it had been made there by a butter taster; his hair was like a half-tanned fox skin, and his whole face was as ragged as a newly picked mill-stone."[17]

"This diet (red clay and blackberries) had given to Ransy a complexion that a corpse would have disdained to own."[18]

"Seth was so notoriously ugly, that his wink was an outrage, and his overtures of love perfect atrocities."[19]

Classic of the ugly man was old Bill Wallis. Flies would not light on his face. When he was ten years old he caught a sight of his reflection in a stream, and ran for his life, hollering for his mammy at every step. Glass an inch thick shattered when he looked into it. His wife practiced kissing the cow before she tried to kiss him.

"His face, generally, had the appearance of a recently healed blister spot. His prominent eyes seemed ready to drop off his face, and were almost guiltless of lids... His mouth — ruby-red — looked as if it had been very lately kicked by a roughly shod mule, after having been originally made by gouging a hole in his face with a nail-grab! The tout ensemble was horribly, unspeakably *ugly!*" [20]

The Ugly Man's climatic triumph was over lightning.

"... I got ketcht in a hurricane; it was blowin' like the devil, and the thunder and lightnin' was tremenjus — so I git under a big red-oak, and thar I sot twell the lightnin' struck it! I was leanin' agin the tree when the bolt come down, shiverin' and splinterin' all before it. It hit me right here — and then —"

"Good heavens! did *lightning* disfigure your face so?"

"Disfigure? hell no! The lightnin' struck right here, as I was sayin', and then — IT GLANCED!" [21]

An earthy humor unmistakably was the crude and boister-ous laughter of the pioneers and their descendants. The huge joke that an ugly man or a corpse provided, a century ago, is today an obsolete fashion of humor. Yet this fashion indicates the underlying vigor and robustiousness of frontier life, in the guise of callousness and crudity. The laughter, as the life, was not gentle nor over-refined.

(A traveller comes upon a small town, is horrified to see a dead horse with his forequarters jammed against the general store and his lifeless rider lying nearby, while the townspeople sit around apatheti-cally. Distressfully he seeks the circumstances.)

"... Has this man a wife and children?" inquired I.

"No children that I knows on," answered a female, who was sitting on the ground a short distance from the dead man, smoking com-posedly.

"He has a wife, then?" I remarked. "What will be her feelings when she learns the fatal termination of this most unfortunate race?"

"Yes," sighed the female, "it was an unfortunate race. Poor man! he lost the whiskey."

"Do you happen to know his wife? Has she been informed of the untimely death of her husband?" were my next inquiries.

"Do I *know* her? Has she been informed of his death?" said the woman. "Well, I reckon you ain't acquainted about these parts. *I* am the unfortunate widder."

"You madam! You the wife of this man who has been so untimely cut off?" I exclaimed, in astonishment.

"Yes, and what about it?" said she. "Untimely cut off? His throat's cut, that's all, by that 'tarnal sharp end of a log; and as for it's being untimely, I don't know but it's as well now as any time — he warn't of much account, nohow!"

She resumed her smoking, and we resumed our journey . . .[22]

Maybe the frontier laughed so uncouthly because it was branded uncouth. Somewhat in the manner of an oat-sowing youth, it boasted of its shortcomings. Delicacy was the password in the genteel literature of the period; in the vigorous newspaper humor of the day it was a word unknown. Barbarous fights were described with a relish for gruesome detail. Squeamishness was a subject for derision.

"I kept my thumb in his eye, and was just going to give it a twist and bring the peeper out, like taking up a gooseberry in a spoon—"[23]

Bullies would keep their thumb-nails oiled and trimmed as sharp as hawk's claws. Ask them why, they would reply, "To feel fur a feller's eyestrings and make him tell the news."[24]

Fighting, hunting and courting were the chief diversions of the frontier; all were equally arduous sport. Undisturbed by Victorian taboo, the story-tellers of the backwoods pictured the cornfed beauty of the backwoods wench as graphically as their ugly men or rough-and-tumble fights. Here is a yarner intriguing his auditor with an account of a beautiful country lass he found sleeping in his bed:

"As I gazed upon her, I thought that I had never witnessed anything more beautiful. From underneath a little night-cap, rivalling the snow in whiteness, fell a stray ringlet over a neck and shoulders of alabaster."

"Well!" said the excited Captain, giving his chair another hitch.

"Never did I look upon a bust more perfectly formed. I took hold of the coverlid and softly pulled it down —"

"Well!" said the captain, betraying the utmost excitement.

"To her waist —"

"*Well!!*" said the captain, dropping the paper, and renewing the position of his legs.

"She had on a night dress, buttoned up before, but softly I opened the first two buttons —"

"Well!!!" said the captain, wrought to the highest pitch of excitement.

"And then, ye gods! what a sight to gaze upon! Pshaw, words fail. Just then —"

"WELL!!!!" said the captain, hitching his chair right and left, and squirting his tobacco juice against the stove so that it fairly fizzed.

"I thought I was taking a mean advantage of her, so I covered her up, seized my coat and boots, and went and slept in another room!"

"It's a lie!" shouted the excited captain, jumping up and kicking over his chair. "IT'S A LIE!!"[25]

Frontier humor was a broad humor; truly the frontier yarn was often as broad as it was long. Alongside the correct magazines of the day, such as the then currently popular "Godey's Lady's Book," the racy newspaper columns form a most acceptable contrast. Spicy comments and observations enliven the newspaper sketches:

"Es I swung my eyes over the crowd, I thought quiltins, managed in a moral an' sensible way, truly am good things — good fur free drinking, good fur free eating, good fur free huggin, good fur free dancin, good fur free fitin, an' goodest ove all fur poperlatin' a country fast."[26]

"Git up, Sall; all those fellows couldn't a seed more ef you was married to 'em all."[27]

"Sich a bosom! Jis' think of two snow balls wif a strawberry buttended intu bof on em . . ."[28]

(Old Mrs. Bass severely criticizes the younger generation of woman for the new trend in bustles) "— makes 'em look bigger behin' than afore — for all the world like an 'oman was sorter in a curious way behind."[29]

"Widders am a speshul means George, fur ripenin green men, killin off weak ones, and makin 'tarnally happy the sound ones."[30]

"Men were made a-purpose jis to eat, drink, an' fer stayin' awake in the early part of the nite; an' wimmen were made to cook the vittils, mix the spirits, an' help the men do the stayin' awake."[31]

The gusty, lusty frontier sketch is alive and fresh today as it was in the newspapers and almanacs of a hundred years ago. It is the most distinctive and enduring strain of American humor, and though partaking of characteristics in common with the national blend — the American penchant for exaggeration and burlesque, the American delight in mocking the finer things and the higher places — it remains unique in the compost of its nature-spattered imagery, its sly delineation of the quirks and eccentricities of frontier folk, its vibrant realism and virility.

II

The literature of frontier humor died with the Civil War. The newspaper sketches changed; the hunting yarns and tall stories of the frontier gave way to the new genre of the professional funny men. Misspelling replaced dialect, and the national scene the local; the flavor of the folk disappeared.

American humor swept on to new forms of satire and ridicule; yet the folk quality that underlay the humor of the Old Southwest rose again to the surface in loose tall tale narratives that cradled a burlesque mythology. An expanding body of humorous folk tales traversed the frontier and reached print, as always, through the medium of the interested observer in the backwoods. In the formula of the ante-bellum newspaper sketch the naive campfire yarn had been metamorphosed into a rather sophisticated literary anecdote in which the touch was often delicately subtle and telling, in spite of the veneer of crudity. In later appearances of the tall tale the transmission tends to be more direct, but the oral source and the primitive scene are discernible in any literary revelation of the frontier sense of humor, whether in journalistic sketch or local color vignette or records of folklore and legend. Observe how, in that most exaggerative of all humorous newspaper sketches, "The Big Bear of Arkansas," the story-teller within the story is interrupted to let the backwoodsman subdue the dandy in the time-honored oral joust.

"What seasons of the year do your hunts take place?" inquired a gentlemanly foreigner who, from some peculiarities of his baggage, I suspected to be an Englishman, on some hunting expedition, probably at the foot of the Rocky Mountains.

"The season for bar hunting, stranger," said the man of Arkansaw, "is generally all the year round, and the hunts take place about as regular."[32]

The imaginative fantasies of the frontier are indissolubly linked with the oral method. Frontier story telling approached a folk art, uniting graphic improvisation with the narrative technique of the skilled raconteur. Traditionary tales infiltrated through the backwoods with the force of a folk tradition.

There is a yarn that concerns a man and a bear in savage tussle. The wife looks on, an interested spectator. "Go it, man; go it, bear," she cheers. "This is the fust fight I ever seed that I didn't care which won!" The yarn is recast in Yankee dialect by Rowland Robinson, skillful limner of Vermont backwoods folk; it finds its way into a Joe Miller joke book under the heading "Life in Kentucky;" it is in the repertoire of at least one famous frontier story-teller, Abe Lincoln.[33]

A hunter cannot shoot a deer which is running around a mountain, or an Indian who is hiding behind a tree. So, according to a writer of North Carolina frontier humor, a folklore student of the Kentucky backwoods, a local color fictionist of the middle western frontier, he bends his gun and fires a crooked shot.[34]

Invention and tradition were never more successfully coupled than in the tale of the miraculous bag: a hunter fires his last shot at a fat bear; the recoil knocks him into the river, and he comes up with his pockets full of fish; a button pops from his trousers and lands in a rabbit's eye, or in a deer's mouth and chokes him; the bullet ricochets into a covey of quail or a brace of red squirrels. Versions of this familiar brag are reported by George Lyman Kittredge in New England almanacs, by Vance Randolph among Ozark Mountain windies, by Earl Collins in Missouri folk tales, and they creep apocryphally into the John Henry and Paul Bunyan cycles.[35]

And so, through unnumbered retellings, key tales multiplied and passed into a homely comic poetry. At whatever point along the lonely frontier men close to the soil gathered, tall tales were told — among Tennessee mountaineers, hunters in the canebrakes of Kentucky, flatboatmen on the Mississippi, cowpunchers in Texas and Arizona, oil-drillers in Oklahoma, fur trappers in the Rockies, loggers in the North Woods, farmers in upstate New York and backwoods New England, Maine tars and Cape Cod salts—and still are told today where frontier folkways yet persist, among miners, factory workers, hoboes. Visualize, if you can, a knot of hard-bitten, weather-beaten pioneers, grouped around the campfire or in the bunkshanty, solemnly attentive to the reminiscent vagaries of some grizzled Nestor, interrupting occasionally to wrangle over some absurd point or insert a weird conceit. It is the frontiersman's fun, his escape, his opportunity to create. In the warmth and strength of effusion, the delight in the purposeful exaggeration, the multicolored backdrop of the American panorama, there is an unmistakable sameness to the varied versions of the American tall tale.

When the agglutinative process of legend clustered tall tales around a nuclear figure, a rude mythology was bred. A host of regional demigods arose to bestride the forests, the plains and the rivers, each individually splashed with local color, yet all stamped with the one die of the American myth-forge. The generic figure is the eccentric frontiersman glorified, a braggart and a brawler, picaresque, earth-tainted, whimsically grotesque, not quite superman or hero or god in the accepted sense, but a comic embodiment of all three, inevitably spawned in the oral humor of elemental men. Each legendary titan is etched with the same bold, ludicrous strokes, molded into the same gargantuan, preposterous outlines. He may be the cowboys' giant in the far Southwest, Pecos Bill:

"After walking a couple of hundred miles Pecos came on a big mountain lion who was just spoiling for a fight. He licked the lion to a fare-you-well, then put his saddle on the big cat and went whoopin' and yellin' down the canyon, swingin' his rattlesnake quirt.

"Soon he saw a chuck wagon with a bunch of cowboys setting round it. He rode up to the feed-box, splittin' the air with his war-whoops, with that old lion a-screechin', and that snake singin' his rattles. When he came to the fire he grabbed the old cougar by the ear, jerked him back on his haunches, stepped off him, hung his snake around his neck, and looked the outfit over. Them cowboys just sat there sayin' less than nothing.

"Bill was hungry, and seeing a boilerful of beans cooking on the fire scooped up a few handfuls and swallowed them, washing them down with a few gallons of boiling coffee out of the pot. Wiping his mouth on a handful of prickly pear cactus, Bill turned to the cowboys and asked 'Who the hell is boss around here?' A big fellow about eight feet tall, with seven pistols and nine bowie knives in his belt, rose up and taking off his hat, said: 'Stranger, I was, but you be'."[36]

Or he may be the bums' colossus in the Bowery, Big Mose Humphreys:

"Old bums still remember Big Mose. He was 12 feet tall, had feet like East River barges. He used to jump from Manhattan to Jersey, and pick up street cars like orange crates. He had red hair and a red fireman's shirt as big as a tent. When his girl turned him down he went to the South Seas, met an island princess, and never returned to the Bowery. But even now, when a bum finds a good cigar butt, he says, 'Big Mose must of dropped it.' Mose smoked such fine cigars that millionaires used to pop into the gutter to pick up his butts."[37]

Yet not one of this Olympian crew is suitably enshrined in literature. The mythical and mystical frontier that bred this race of blustering demigods is not easily caught in print; the folk spirit becomes diluted, the vernacular of legend transmogrified, and only snatches and fragments of the epic cycles are handed down. Literature has given a dim and shaky reflection of legend.

There is, perhaps, an exception; in the Crockett almanacs we come to a closer view of a full-bodied legendary personality.

The value of the Crockett almanacs is not readily discernible in their original issues, with their close-printed jumble of anecdotes and sketches. But skim off the better stories, group them in their natural pattern, and America's most authentic folk literature emerges: most authentic because, in catching the rhythms of folk speech, the anonymity of the legend method and the supernatural inventions of mythology, the Davy Crockett myth is closest of our scanty legend literatures to the national epics. Infused with the bawdy humor of the frontier, it is, in a way, America's own crude and grotesque epic.

In the Crockett almanacs, frontier humor and legend logically blend. The idiom belongs to the adept anecdotal genre of the humorous newspaper literature rampant before the Civil War; the comic hero conforms to the broad pattern of the American myth-type, the frontier superman. Native fantasy has found native tongue.

★

The trail of frontier humor and legend winds through the backwoods of northern New England, where dry-lipped woodsmen spread Yankee-tinged folk tales of Sam Patch, Sam Slick and Sam Hyde; it skirts past Paul Bunyan's logging camps in the Great Lake pineries, lingers in the far West to catch the deep-throated laughter that echoes to the exploits of Jim Bridger and the mountain men, sweeps down through the Nebraskan plains of Febold Feboldson and the Oklahoma oilfields of Kemp Morgan to wide Texan cattle ranges where cowboys swap yarns of Strap Buckner and Pecos Bill; it retraces the course of the old Indian frontier across Mike Fink's Mississippi to the canebrakes of Kentucky and the pioneer throng, Boone and Crockett, famed Indian fighter Wetzel, half-breed Girty, dare-devil Simon Kenton; it stretches south into the cotton fields where toiling darkies sing ballads of John Henry and Uncle Remus talks of Brer Rabbit, curls through Sut Lovingood's Tennessee along the mountain pockets of the Blue Ridge and the Ozarks where Sol Shell and Windy Bill still tell their tall ones, passes on up Tony Beaver's undiscovered Eel River and beyond, to York State farmers gossiping of John Darling; it meanders along the salt-sprayed coastline to pick up wind-blown yarns of Bowleg Bill the sea-going cowboy and Old Stormalong, king of Yankee sailors. . . .

It is the saga of America, her history and geography and legend and laughter spun into a varicolored epic strand weaving across the continent — sorrowful reminder of an America that is now a dimming memory.

DAVY CROCKETT
AMERICAN COMIC LEGEND

Being a collection of tales and legends on and about

the Mississippi screamer, Salt River roarer and half-

horse, half-alligator hero of the Kentucky canebrakes,

Colonel Crockett himself.

Birth of Crockett

Aunt Ketinah and Uncle Roarious war dreadful tickled when I war born, and thought that thar war never sich a young one sence acorns growed on trees. Aunt Ketinah held up her hands and said I war the very pictur of good luck, for I war so fat that it war as good as a meal's vittles to look at me. She said she knowed that I war cut out to be a great man, and wanted to have the bringing of me up. She said that she would bathe my head every morning with bear's gall, as that are great for bringing forward the intellectures of young sports, and she would have my internal examined every week by the doctor, to see that I war not inclined to the cholera morbus, as that was what her grandmother died on.

As for Uncle Roarious he wanted to see me eat, and so they made a smart chance of whiskey pap for me, and broke two rattle-snakes' eggs in it, and give me it in a spoon made of a buffalo's hoof, and an eagle's leg for a handle. When they seed me swallow they declared that I war the flower of the hull family, and would do more execution with my thumb-nail than any of my posteriors had ever done before me. Arter that, they put me up in a tall tree, and lashed me to the top, so that the wind could swing me about, and that war the cradle in which I war rocked when I war young.

Crockett's Father

Seein that family pictures are goin ahead, I jist thought I'd present my old friends with a real nateral likeness o' my daddy and mammy and cradle. Here you see a pictur o' Davy Crockett Seignior. Now, arn't he a venerable sample of white oak? The old cock's bark is a little wrinkled, but his trunk is so all flinty hard that you can strike fire from it with a sledge hammer. He is now in his One-Hundred and

Forty-Ninth year, and he can look the sun in the face without sneezing. He can grin a hail-storm into sunshine, and with his third crop of teeth he can do all our family grindin.

Crockett's Mother

Now I gin you a genuine portrait of my mammy, in her One-Hundred and Forty-Eighth year, and an all-screamin' glorious gal she is of her age. She can jump a seven rail fence backwards, dance a hole through a double oak floor, spin more wool than one of your steam mills, and smoke up a ton of Kentucky weed in a week. She can crack walnuts for her great grandchildren with her front teeth, and laugh a horse blind. She can cut down a gum tree ten feet around, and steer it across Salt River with her apron for a sail, and her left leg for a rudder.

Crockett's Cradle

The last family portrait I shall give you, is one of the cradle I war rocked in, as large as life. It is just twelve feet long; the body is made out o' the shell of a snapping turtle that weighed six hundred pounds, and the hull of it is varnished with the oil of fifteen rattlesnakes, two hundred years old; the head on it is made of buck's horns, and kivered with wild cat-

4

skins; the rockers are made of the fore teeth of a mammoth that war killed by my great-great-grandfather; the piller is an alligator's hide, stuffed with Indian scalps. In this cradle I war rock'd by water power.

Infant Crockett at the Dinner Table

Arter awhile, I got old enough to eat knife and fork vittles. Then my father and mother sot me on the table, and give me the carving knife. Bear's meat war my favorite, though I took some wild fowl once in a while, jest for a whet. It war thought best to wean me on whiskey: so I had a bladder with a pipe in it, and the bladder was filled with whiskey, and I sucked at the pipe in the most soakoriferous manner; but as

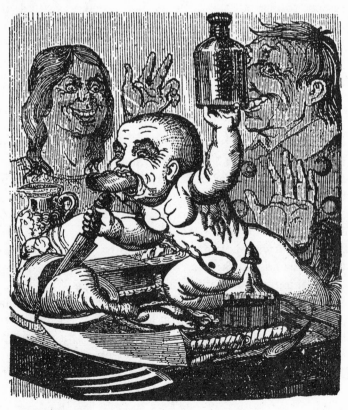

soon as I war weaned, I took to bear's meat in the most rantankerous manner, and made it fly without wings. I would
take up a roasted duck by the neck and gnaw the meat off the
bones before the rest had time to set down to the table; and as
for gravy, I used to drink it. That war one reason that I got to
be so good a speechifer and war sent to Congress. As for mustard, I used to put the meat in one plate and the mustard in the
tother, and arter I had done with my meat, I dove into the
mustard for to give the meat a relish. Half a pint of it war only
a taster. I always took a pint of whiskey and mustard to give
me an appetite for breakfast in the morning. Arter dinner, I
always went 'round the table and licked out all the dishes and
plates, which saved my mother the trouble of washing 'em. My
mother liked it so well, that arter I war grown up, she kept a
tame bear to lick out the dishes, which saved a pesky deal of
trouble, as well as the soap and dish water. At eleven o'clock
I always took a sandwich, which was composed of half a bear's
ham, two spare ribs, a loaf of bread, and a quart of whiskey.

Crockett Growing Up

The fust thing that I can remember ar a bear's snout. It war
a great while ago; but I remember how his long nose looked.
It war at the time I war in my cradle. He poked his snout in
and war jest going to take a piece out of my profile, when my
mother set her peepers on him, and flung a hull bowl of rattlesnake soup on his hinder eend.

But when I war six year old, I begun to hunt varmints. We
had a big dog named Butcher, and I got on his back and sot out
arter small game — my father held up the piece while I fired it
off, and I shot a small chance of varmints the fust year that I
begun. I war considered the wonder of the rising generation,
at hunting, and drinking whiskey. I war arly brought up to
good execution, and once I drew a lead on a fox when I war
only in my seventh year. Arter that I war allowed to sot up to
the table and take my horn of whiskey with big folks, and

every body prophesied that I should be a great man, tho' they didn't forsee that I should be a member of Congress.

I hadn't begun to take out eyes in them arly days, tho' I scratched my mother most beautiful whenever she tried to wash my face.

Likeness of Crockett
When Eight Years Old

Thar, stranger, your folks may talk about thar infant prodigies, precocious juveniles, and all that, and some of these half grown pigs may carry themselves about for a show, but I contend that human nater isn't show-beef, any more than a white baby is a young baboon. Though I war the biggest infant that ever was, and a little the smartest that ever will be, I always war too big to carry my flesh about for a show.

Now thar are a perfect likeness of me when I war eight years old, as large as life, an' almost as nateral. At that time,

I weighed about two hundred pounds an' fourteen ounces, with my shoes off, an' my feet clean, an' stomach empty; and my flesh war so solid that they used to take my body for a roller to level gravel walks with, and my head war used for a grindstone. If they wanted to split a rock in two, all they had to do was to swing me up, hands and heels, to a block an' tackle, by horse power, and then push me backwards an' forwards,—and the way my pate used to make the fire fly, and the cliffs come apart, war about equal to a high pressure airthquake.

If they wanted to sink tree posts in the bed of the river, for budge piers, all they had to do was to jist lower 'em down into the mud, and then let me dive 'em down by jumpin' from one to the other; and the way I used to make thar tallest timbers pop down war a caution.

The first teeth I shed war taken to build our parlour fireplace. My head war not so productive of hair, but it sarved to make all the gals in the house upper beds for the first five years; and I sweat taller enough the first ten years to keep all the neighbors in candle grease. My toe and finger nails used to keep the family in horn buttons.

And how do you think all this great growth war cultivated? Was it unnateral growth, or a "looseness nater," as the scholars say? No sir-ee, not at all, by no means: it war all done up through my parents' Crocketonian system of flesh cultur. For as soon as I war born, they planted me in a rock bed on Thunder Shower Hill, watered me with wild buffaloes' milk, with boiled corn-cobs and tobacco leaves, and I sprouted as suddenaciously as the island of St. Helena, which they say sprouted up out of the sea in a single night.

Crockett's First Love

I must confess that I've had a smart chance of sweethearts in my days. The first one that I ever had war the pride of old Kaintuck, and lived up in Gum Hollow, on Goose Creek. Every winter she fatted up on bear's meat, so that when she turned out in spring, she war bigger round than a whiskey bar-

8

rel; and when I put my arms 'round the cretur, it war like hugging a bale of cotton. Her two legs war like a couple o' hemlock trees, and when she sneezed it shook the leaves from the trees, and skeered setting hens off thar eggs.

She war a very virchus gal, too; for when a Yankee pedlar undertook to come the soft soap over her, she kotched him by the heels and poked him up the chimbly till his head come out the top. Thar never war a gal that liked me as she did, till I had a few words with her brother; and arter I had put one of his eyes in my pocket, she thought I didn't act like a friend to the family.

Her name war Florinda Fury, and she used to set off for church meeting that war held up in Deer Meetin' House, every Sunday morning, carrying her vittles with her. She always took a rifle, to argufy with the varmints when she met 'em on the road; and sometimes she carried a rooster in her pocket, as they used to have a cock-fight in the meetin' house arter sarvice war over. Finally she married Ralph Leaf, a fifteenth cozzen of mine, and the same gentleman what 'lectioneered for me when I war up for Congress, as he said that it would be an honor to him to have a relation in Congress.

The Colonel Swallows
a Thunderbolt

Thar are a great many kinds of larning. I found it out when I went to Kongress. Thar are your mattymatticks, your jommy-trees, your sighentifficks, and your axletrissity.

I knows nothing about the other ones, but the axletrissity is a screamer. Thar war a feller in Washington that put the thunder and litening into glass bottles, and when a feller had the roomatiz, or the Saint Vitals dance, he would put the axletrissity into his corpse jist like pouring whiskey into a powder horn, and it cured him as clean as a barked tree. So I seed how 'twas done; and intarmined whenever ennything ailed me to try it, only I didn't keer about the bottles, for I thort I could

9

jist as well take the litening in the raw state as it come from the clouds. I had been used to drink out of the Mississippy without a cup, and so I could take the litening without the bottles and whirligigs that belongs to an axletrissityfying machine.

It fell out that some two years arter I had been to see this axletrissity, I got a leetle in love with a pesky smart gal in our clearing, and I knowed it war not rite, seeing I war a married man. So I combobbolated on the subject, and at last I resisted that I would explunctificate my passions by axletrissity, by bringing it right on the heart and driving the love out of it.

So I went out into the forest one arternoon when thar war a pestiferous thunder gust. I opened my mouth, so that the axletrissity might run down and hit my heart, to cure it of love. I stood so for an hour, and then I seed a thunderbolt a-comin', and I dodged my mouth right under it, and plump it went into my throat. My eyes! it war as if seven buffaloes war kicking in my bowels. My heart spun round amongst my insides like a grindstone going by steam, but the litening went clean through me, and tore my trowsers off as it come out. I had a sore gizzard for two weeks, and my inwards war so hot that I use to eat raw vittals for a month arterward, and it would be cooked before it got fairly down my throat.

I have never felt love since.

Crockett's Wonderful Escape
Up Niagara Falls

You've all heard o' the Injun's great feat of steerin' safely down ole Niagara Falls in a canoe. Well, I confess, the red crittur did show a pretty considerable majority of pluck an' dexterity, but it took me to beat him all to the very smallest bit o' nothin', for I steered an alligator right up the etarnal roarin' thunder water, jist as slick as a stream o' wind going up a chimney.

I'll tell you how it happened: — you see as how, during the last revolution in Canada, I paid an express visit to my friend,

10

and brother hero, General Pappinou,* the great hull-souled
leader an' ful blooded French Yankee patriot. He were then

*Louis Joseph Papineau was leader of the insurgent French Canadian party
which openly rebelled against British rule in 1837, and accordingly found sympathy in the United States. It was as a participant in the Papineau rebellion that
the historical prototype of the mythical Paul Bunyan is, supposedly, first recorded.

11

quartered a few miles below the falls, an' I steered across to him on my great pet Alligator, "Long Mississippi." But the tarnal Royalists no sooner found that I were beyond the lines of Uncle Sam, than they seemed to dread a suddenacious destruction from me; and one night while I were taking a comfortable snooze with my head resting on the neck of "Long Mississippi," the tarnal cowards marched down with all thar forces to surprise an' capture me.

For the first time in the hull o' my life I war caught napping, for the tarnal sly critturs surrounded me fifteen double all round. For fear of the patriots, they concluded to march me up to thar fort near the falls by water: so they manned their boats on the right, and part on 'em led; the next follered behind, leaving me in the middle mounted in the curl o' my alligator's tail. Soon as we got close to the falls, the leading party pulled close to the Canada side, with a tarnal tantilization shout o' triumph, thinking of course, that I must foller 'em, or get drowned in ole Niagara's all creation of a spout.

But by all go-ahead-itiveness they were most tarnally mistaken, for I jist tickled up the old alligator with my toe, twisted his tail around my body, put my thumb to my nose, an' we walked up the great hill o' water as slick as a wild cat up a white oak. And the way my pet an' me grinned "no go" an' Yankee tantilization at these pets of Queen Victoria set 'em all to bitin' their guns and swords with teetotal vexation. By way of a parting salute, my alligator sent such a cloudburst of old Niagara's cold water upon 'em, that they all cut stick like so many half drowned turkies from a spring shower, thinking that the hull entire cataract was coming to baptise 'em Christians and Republicans. My pet an' me shot up the rapids about as fast as a roughshod rocket, and landed on Uncle Sam's side, amid a salute of five hundred double barrelled rifles in honor of Colonel Crockett and his amphibious pet cataract navigator.

Crockett and Ben Hardin Make Their Escape from a Tornado by Mounting a Streak of Lightning

Every one has heard of the all-sweepin', smashin' tarnal Tornado at Natchez, but they never heered o' the particulars o' my escape from it along with Ben Hardin. I'll jist tell you how it war.

You see, Ben Hardin and me war setting at the starn of a steamer talkin politics about as loud as low thunder, when, rather suddenaciously, I heard a distant roarin', something like the voice of old Niagara when the wind blows up steam.

"Hello, thar's a storm comin," says the Captin.

"No, it's a steamer," says Ben.

"Bah! it's only the echo of our voices," says I.

But the noise got bigger, and the water begun to squirm about like a stirred-up punch bowl, and the boats begun playin' rock an' seesaw at such an etarnal rate that even I couldn't hold 'em still. Then came a roar that would have made old Niagara sound like a kitten; the trees walked out by the roots, and danced about like injins; the houses come apart; the people screamed all sorts o' frightened-to-death-ativeness, and some of them appeared to be going up to heaven heels foremost. This appeared to be the beginning on it, and Ben and me thought it was time to be off; the boats begun to play smash with one another, and the ribs of ourn got stove in clar to the biler. Fortunately, a stray streak of lightnin' came passin' along, so jist as it come I grabbed it by the fork, and sprung on it. Ben follered, and held on to my hair; I greased it a leetle with a bottle of rattlesnake taller, and the way we streaked it, and left the tornado behind, was astonishin' to all natur.

Crockett's Opinion of a Thunder Storm

Folks may talk and crow as much as they can about the roar of Niagara, the growlin' o' the sea, an' the barkin' o' them big iron bull dogs called cannons, but give me a hull team of storm-brewed thunder, an' your other natral music is no more than a penny trumpet to the hand organ of a hurrycane. By the great bein' above, a reglar round roarin' savage peal o' thunder is the greatest treat in all creation! It sets everything but a coward an' a darned culprit shouting in the very heart and soul till both on 'em swell so etarnal big with nat'ral glorification that one feels as if he could swoller the entire creation at a gap, hug the hull universe at once, then go to sleep so full of thunder glory, that he'll wake up with his head an entire electrical machine, and his arms a teetotal thunderbolt. Jist give me a touch o' this sort of natral music afore I go to

14

sleep; arter I wake up, I feel my bump of veneration for old mammy nater so all-mountain big, that I can kneel down an' hug old Mississippi, bust a big rock, an' feel strong enough to do the duty of an entire saw mill.

Crockett's Original and Aboriginal Descent of Mont-Blanc

A few years ago I took a Rocky-Mountain Injun for a companion with a determination to visit Europe, solely for the purpose of climbing up and exploring them three hundred feet icicles and glaciers in Switzerland, and that all-terrifying and natural snow-steeple, Mont-Blanc. I've heerd a good deal of talk about the difficulty of that tall walk, and although it seemed an uphillish sort of business, it was not half so much trouble to me and my Rocky-Mountain Injun as scaling Cloud-Cliff in Oregon when it is greased with sleet.

Well, we got up to the top all right, swallowed a few snow-balls, and washed them down with galvanized whiskey, gave three loud crows for Uncle Sam, and then started down — when suddenaciously we smelt a loud shake, and heard a roar loud enough to scare a thunderbolt. I asked what it meant, and a guide of a party of travellers called it an Avalanche. He said that the mountain was caving out, and if we started to descend we would all get caved in.

"Avalanche or no," said I, "here goes a launch down to the bottom afore caving-in comes."

So I just took and placed my copper-colored comrade sled-fashion on a good streak of snow, and we slid and coasted from snow-top clean down to grass as soon as wink, leaving old Mr. Avalanche rumbling and grumbling behind, completely distanced by the launch of Col. Crockett & Co.

Crockett's Morning Hunt

One January morning it was so all-screwen-up cold that the forest trees war so stiff that they couldn't shake, and the very day-break froze fast as it war tryin' to dawn. The tinder-box in my cabin would no more ketch fire than a sunk raft at the bottom o' the sea. Seein' that daylight war so far behind time, I thought creation war in a fair way for freezin' fast.

"So," thinks I, "I must strike a leetle fire from my fingers, light my pipe, travel out a few leagues, and see about it."

Then I brought my knuckles together like two thunder clouds, but the sparks froze up afore I could begin to collect 'em — so out I walked, and endeavored to keep myself unfriz by goin' at a hop, step and jump gait, and whistlin' the tune of "fire in the mountains!" as I went along in three double quick time. Well, arter I had walked about twenty-five miles up the peak o' Daybreak Mill, I soon discovered what war the matter. The airth had actually friz fast in her axis, and couldn't turn round; the sun had got jammed between two cakes o' ice under the wheels, an' thar he had bin shinin' and workin' to get loose, till he friz fast in his cold sweat.

"C-r-e-a-t-i-o-n!" thought I, "this are the toughest sort o' suspension, and it musn't be endured—somethin' must be done, or human creation is done for."

It war then so antedeluvian and premature cold that my upper and lower teeth an' tongue war all collapsed together

16

as tight as a friz oyster. I took a fresh twenty pound bear off o' my back that I'd picked up on the road, an' beat the animal agin the ice till the hot ile began to walk out on him at all sides. I then took an' held him over the airth's axes, an' squeezed him till I thaw'd 'em loose, poured about a ton on it over the sun's face, give the airth's cog-wheel one kick backward, till I got the sun loose — whistled "Push along, keep movin'!" an' in about fifteen seconds the airth gin a grunt, and begun movin'—the sun walked up beautiful, salutin' me with sich a wind o' gratitude that it made me sneeze. I lit my pipe by the blaze o' his top-knot, shouldered my bear, an' walked home, introducin' the people to fresh daylight with a piece of sunrise in my pocket, with which I cooked my bear steaks, an' enjoyed one o' the best breakfasts I had tasted for some time. If I didn't, jist wake some mornin' and go with me to the office o' sunrise!

Crockett's Uncle

My old Uncle Zebulon war the capting of the Thunder and Lightning Screamers, a company that war raised in old Kaintuck, in the time of the war. He war born in Crab Apple Clearing, and his mother used to scrape him down with chestnut burs to make him tough. He had the meazles and small pox and kine pox all at once, with the seven years itch, and that hurt his beauty a little. He swam across the Massissippy when he war seven years old, and licked his grandmother when

17

he war only eight. I haint no doubt he would have been sent to Congress, but in them days, when he war young, it warn't the fashion to teech young fokes to read or rite; so I war the only one sent to Congress. Uncle Zeb died at last of eating too hearty of a pie made of crocodile's tripe; it war a dish that he war pesky fond of.

Crockett's Aunt

My Aunt war the sister of Pine Rook, the most rantankerous fighter in the valley of the Massissippy. She war raised in Pine Clearing; when she war a child, her pap war made of rattlesnake brains and maple sap, well peppered, and biled into a jelly. She growed so fast on that, that she rassled with a nigger in her thirteenth year, and threw him. My uncle war thar when she did it, and he fell in love with her right off, and made her a present of a tame bear, and two eyes that he had gouged out at the last election. She dried the eyes and hung one in each ear, and wore them to church. On the day she war married, she chased a crocodile half a mile.

The Indian and Crockett's Grandmother

You see my Grandmother was an all-standin tough gal, in her 120th year; but she'd a damned stubborn cough, and so echoaciously loud, that it used to set the cider barrels rolling about the cellar, and her only relief was to go into the woods once a day and chaw hickory limbs.

Well, one mornin' while she was settin' on a stump, and using up the last limb o' hickory, a tarnal sneak of a 'tater nosed Injun walked most audaciously up to her, collared her by the cap, and started preparing his execution iron in true Injun valor to carve off old Granny's top knot. Now Granny, being a regular fotched up Kentuck gal, didn't mind her scalp no more than a cherry-stone; but her family cap war of the true Martha Washington's pattern, and she'd sooner parted with life, cough and all.

So she hung out her eyes at him obstinaciously wicked, while he squinted at her, scalpaciously cruel. Then he grabbed her by the cap, hair and all; Granny bit her hickory and spit it at him; he flourished his execution iron sarcledicularly, and giving a most valorous and romantic war-whoop, war just goin' to hull-scalp Granny, cap and all — when she give one o' her all shakin' coughs that sent the red nigger rollin' in the leaves as if he war struck by the bare foot of an earthquake. He leaned agin a tree, an' shivered an' panted like a steam bellows, an' then tried to cough back at Granny. But it warn't no use, he couldn't cough back her cough. So he cut his arm, drunk a little warm blood as a renovator, an' grinned all colours of antymosity at Granny.

The old gal set still, extendin' her left eye at him, and chawin' hickory considerably. Old 'Tater Nose thort this war a cough producer, so he cut off a hickory limb and begun chawin' it like a bark machine. Arter that he thort he'd try its power, so he give Granny three or four jumpin' coughs; Granny grinned an' gummed at him, and didn't mind 'em a sneeze, jist bit away at her hickory, now an' then spittin' a cheekful at him. But the Injun war still detarmined to have a drink of her vital revolutionary sap, so he crawled towards her, and got as fur as a holler log that he held fast to to breathe by.

Then Granny's revolution begun to rise in her at the rate of old '76, and she settled upon coughin' 'Tater Nose to his coffin instanterly—so she jist walked up neat to the log, give ahem! or two by way of introduction to the operation, an' drawin' up her hickory life basket, give another cough that would have silenced a forty-eight pound cannon. And if that same red nigger didn't roll rite into the holler of a log about as slick as a corpse into a coffin, then petrify me for grave stones. Granny walked safely home with her hickory, and he died of the full-gallop consumption. If he didn't then tar my hide for Injun moccasins.

Mrs. Crockett Beating Up Mike Fink

You've all on you heered of Mike Fink, the celebrated, an' self-created, an' never to be mated, Mississippi roarer, snag-lifter, and flatboat skuller. Well, I knowed the critter all round, an' upside down; he war purty fair amongst squaws, catfish, an' big niggers, but when it come to walkin' into wildcats, bars, or alligators, he couldn't hold a taller candle to my young son, Hardstone Crockett.

I'll never forget the time he tried to scare my wife, Mrs. Sally Ann Thunder Ann Whirlwind Crockett. You see, the critter had tried all sorts of ways to scare her, but he had no more effect on her than droppin' feathers on a barn floor. At last he bet me a dozen wildcats that he would appear to her an' scare her teeth loose an' her toe nails out of joint.

So the varmint one night arter a big freshet took and crept into an old alligator's skin, and met Mrs. Crockett jist as she was taken an evening's walk. He spread open the mouth of the critter, an' made sich a holler howl that he nearly scared himself out of the skin. Mrs. Crockett didn't care any more for that, nor the alligator skin, than she would for a snuff of lightnin, but when Mike got a leetle too close, and put out his paws with the idea of an embrace, then I tell you what, her indignation rose a little bit higher than a Mississippi flood. She throwed a flash of eye-lightnin upon him that made it clear daylight for half an hour, but Mike thinkin' of the bet an' his fame for courage, wagged his tail an' walked still closer; Mrs. Crockett out with a little teethpick, and with a single swing of it sent the hull head and neck flyin' fifty feet off, the blade jist shavin' the top of Mike's head.

Then seein' what it war, she throwed down her teethpick, rolled up her sleeves, and battered poor Fink so that he fainted away in his alligator skin. And he war so all-scaren mad, when he come to, that he swore he had been chawed up and swallered by an alligator.

Davy's Sister Doing Good

My sister Comfort war one of the go-to-meetin' gals, and one of the finest samples of Christianity an' womananity that I ever seed — I says it myself. She swallowed religion hull, and fed on that an' do good-a-tiveness all the days of her life, till she war a parfect model of a natural saint.

She could preach a few too. Her pulpit was the rock, an' her sacrament the pure nat'ral element of Adam; her words would make the coldest individual's heart open like a clam in hot water, and a reperbate's hair stand straight up and bow to her. And when she sung a psalm you'd a thought all the trees in creation war organ pipes, and a harrycane war blowin' the bellows. She has put her tracks an' her tracts all the way from the Alleghany to the Rocky Mountains; she is always on hand, with her heart, arms, an' pockets open, an' has been the travellers' sun, star, an' salvation, for the last three years in the Rocky Mountains. She has worn out seven of her nine constitutions, using up three consumptions, and four fever an' agues in saving travellers from freezing, famine, wolves an' vultures.

The biggest heap of good she ever done was when she walked the frozen bank of Columby river for fifteen days, livin' on nothin' but pure hope, to hunt up the fifteen men lost in Col. Fremont's caravan that was scattered by a snow storm. And that ar gal never rested head nor foot till she explored the hull country, rocks, ravines, an' holler logs, stickin' as true to the chase as an alligator, till she found 'em, and piloted 'em safe to Californy.

Crockett's Daughters

I always had the praise o' raisin the tallest and fattest, and sassyest gals in all America. They can out-run, out-jump, out-fight, and out-scream any crittur in creation; and for scratchin', thar's not a hungry painter, or a patent horse-rake can hold a claw to 'em.

The oldest one growed so etarnally tall that her head had got nearly out o' sight, when she got into an all-thunderin' fight with a thunder storm that stunted her growth, and now I am afraid that she'll never reach her natural size. Still, it takes a hull winter's weavin' to make her walkin' and bed clothes; and when she goes to bed, she's so tarnal long, and sleeps so sound, that we can only waken her by degrees, and that's by chopping fire wood on her shins.

An' I guess I shall never forget how all horrificaciously flumexed a hull party of Indians war, the time they surprised and seized my middle darter, Thebeann, when she war out gatherin' birch bark, to make a canoe. The varmints knew as soon as they got hold of her that she war one of my breed, by her thunderbolt kickin', and they determined to cook half of her and eat the other half alive, out of revenge for the many lickin's I gin 'em. At last they concluded to tie her to a tree, and kindle a fire around her. But they couldn't come it, for while they war gone for wood, a lot of painters that war looking on at the cowardly work, war so gal-vanised an' pleased with the gal's true grit that they formed a guard around her, and wouldn't allow the red niggers to come within smellin' distance; they actually gnawed her loose, an' 'scorted her half way home.

But the youngest o' my darters takes arter me, and is of the regular earthquake natur. Her body's flint rock, her soul's lightnin, her fist is a thunderbolt, and her teeth can out-cut any steam-mill saw in creation. She is a parfect infant prodigy, being only six years old; she has the biggest foot and widest mouth in all the west, and when she grins, she is splendifferous; she shows most beautiful intarnals, and can scare a flock o' wolves to total terrifications.

Well, one day, my sweet little infant was walking in the woods, and amusing herself by picking up walnuts, and cracking them with her front grindstones, when suddenaciously she stumbled over an almitey great hungry he-barr. The critter seein' her fine red shoulders bare, sprung at her as if determined to feast upon Crockett meat. He gin her a savaggerous hug, and was jist about biting a regular buss out on her cheek, when the child, resentin' her insulted vartue, gin him a kick with her south fist in his digestion that made him hug the arth instanterly. Jist as he war a-comin' to her a second time, the little gal grinned sich a double streak o' blue lightnin into his mouth that it cooked the critter to death as quick as think. She brought him home for dinner.

She'll be a thunderin' fine gal when she gets her nateral growth, if her stock o' Crockett lightnin don't burst her biler, and blow her up.

Death of Crockett

Thar's a great rejoicin' among the bears of Kaintuck, and the alligators of the Mississippi rolls up thar shining ribs to the sun, and has grown so fat and lazy that they will hardly move out of the way for a steamboat. The rattlesnakes come up out of thar holes and frolic within ten foot of the clearings, and the foxes goes to sleep in the goose-pens. It is bekase the rifle of Crockett is silent forever, and the print of his moccasins is found no more in our woods. His old fox-skin cap hangs up in the cabin, and every hunter, whether he are a Puke, a Wolverine, or a Sucker, never looks at it without turnin' away his head and droppin' a salt tear.

Luke Wing entered the cabin the other day and took down old Killdevil to look at it. The muzzle was half stopped up with rust, and a great green spider run out of it and made his escape in the cracks of the wall. The varmints of the forest will fear it no more. His last act to defend it, war when the poor gallant Kurnill drew a lead on a pesky Mexican and brought him down. Crockett went to put "Big Butcher" into another, and the feller on the ground turned half over, and stuck a knife into him. Another come up behind and run his bayonet into Crockett's back, for the cretur would as soon have faced a hundred live mammoths as to have faced Crockett at any time.

Down fell the Kurnill like a lion struck by thunder and lightning. He never spoke again. It war a great loss to the country, and the world, and to ole Kaintuck in particklar. Thar were never known such a member of Congress as Crockett, and never will be agin. The painters and bears will miss him, for he never missed them.

He died like a member o' Congress ought to die. While he war about to do his country some sarvice, and raise her name as high as her mountains, he war cut down in the prime o' life, and at a time when he war most wanted. His screams and yells are heard no more, and the whole country are clouded with a darkness for the gallant Kurnill. He war an ornament to the forest, and war never known to refuse his whiskey to a stranger. When he war alive, it war most beautiful to hear his scream coming through the forest; it would turn and twist itself into some of the most splendifferous knots, and then untie itself and keep on till it got clar into nowhere.

But he are a dead man now, and if you want to see old Kaintuck's tears, go thar, and speak o' her gallant Kurnill, and thars not a human but what will turn away and go behind some tree and dry up thar tears. He are dead now, and may he rest forever and a day arter.

"Go Ahead" Reader

Arter the great fuss the public have made about an individual of my humble pretensions, and the mighty deal of attention and good cheer which I have received in all sections of the country, where I have been ahead, my heart has swelled as big as a Bison's, with pure gratitude. To repay all this, I mean to amuse them with some of my adventures with the wild varmints and colts of the West, and with adventures of the backwoodsmen generally. Owing to the partiality of my fellow citizens, I have been made a Congressman, and am from home (at Washington) half the year; but should any of my readers find me at home on the Big Clover Creek, Tennessee, they shall be treated with a good racoon pie, and bush eels (i.e. rattlesnakes) fried in butter—which are dishes my wife cooks to perfection. They shall have the softest white oak log to sit on, and the best bearskin to sleep on, which my house affords. I will take them out on a coon hunt, show 'em how to tree a catamount, and take a blizzard at a bear. They can take a walk in my crabapple orchard, and see the alligator pear trees. And as a plain matter-of-fact, I will convince them that I can run faster,— jump higher,— squat lower,— dive deeper,— stay longer under,— and come out drier, than any man in the whole country.

Speech of Colonel Crockett in Congress

Mr. Speaker:

"Who—Who—Whoop—Bow—Wow—Wow—Yough. I say, Mr. Speaker; I've had a speech in soak this six months, and it has swelled me like a drowned horse; if I don't deliver it I shall burst and smash the windows. The gentleman from Massachusetts talks of summing up the merits of the question, but I'll sum up my own. In one word I'm a screamer, and have got the roughest racking horse, the prettiest sister, the surest rifle and the ugliest dog in the district. I'm a leetle the savagest crittur you ever did see. My father can whip any man in Kentucky, and I can lick my father. I can outspeak any man on this floor, and give him two hours start. I can run faster, dive deeper, stay longer under, and come out drier, than any chap this side the big Swamp. I can outlook a panther and outstare a flash of lightning, tote a steamboat on my back and play at rough and tumble with a lion, with an occasional kick from a zebra. To sum up all in one word — *I'm a horse*. Goliah was a pretty hard colt but I could choke him. I can take the rag off — frighten the old folks — astonish the natives — and beat the Dutch all to smash — make nothing of sleeping under a blanket of snow — and don't mind being frozen more than a rotten apple.

"Congress allows lemonade to the members and has it charged under the head of stationary — I move also that whiskey be allowed under the item of fuel. For bitters I can suck away at a noggin of aquafortis, sweetened with brimstone, stirred with a lightning rod, and skimmed with a hurricane. I've soaked my head and shoulders in Salt River, so much that I'm always corned. I can walk like an ox, run like a fox, swim like an eel, yell like an Indian, fight like a devil, spout like an earthquake, make love like a mad bull, and swallow an Injun whole without choking if you butter his head and pin his ears back."

A Shooting Match

One spell, when I lived in Illinois, I heerd tell of a game of cards that was played after a fashion that's worth telling on, and so I'll give it to my reader just as I heerd it, and if it ain't true, why he got it as cheap as I did, barring having to pay for the Almanac that's got it in.

You are to understand there was to be a great shooting match in them parts, and amongst the rest was a Sucker come up from the south part of the State, a real Indian-hater that had cut many a bullet in two against an Indian's tomahawk, along with a reg'lar built Red Horse from Kentuck, and a Buckeye that shot out the tongue of a crow that was disturbing divine service on a Sunday, at the distance of a hundred yards on the wing. Well, these three all set out together to go to the shooting match. On the way, they got into a dispute about who could shoot the best, and finally they agreed to try their hand at a small sapling, distant about twelve yards. Well, the Sucker fired first by right, as he was in his native state. He missed the tree, owing to the ball hitting a mosquito's leg in its progress, which made it glance a fraction. Kentuck next took aim. He didn't hit the tree, but lamed a caterpillar that was crawling on the bark. Buckeye then poised his rifle, but took no aim, let her off slap; his ball struck the sapling right in the middle, so pat that the tree screamed right out! Buckeye then crowed and jumped up as high as his head, and offered to bet a barrel of whiskey he'd hit the sapling nine times out of ten.

So they kept up firing till all their powder was gone, and so they concluded it was no use to go to the shooting match, and they set down and begun to play cards on the stump of a tree. But before they had finished the game, night came on, and they being in want of light, set fire to the surrounding trees and lit up the forests in place of candles. Men of such exalted views would surely comb their head with nothing less than a hickory scrag, and drink out of nothing less than a river!

The Bully of Salt River

The bully of Salt River war named Skippoweth Branch. He slept in his hat, chawed his vittles with his foreteeth, and could scream through his nose. He sunned himself in a thunder storm, went to meeting on two horses, never turned out for man or beast, and was sworn to lick everything he saw, except his own father and mother. He would walk ten miles, at any time of day or night, for a fight. He called himself the great oak that grows half its length underground, and turns up its roots unexpected. He sometimes took the name of floating iron and melted pewter, red hot cannon balls, and Big Snag of the Desert. He said he lived on the mountains and ate thunder, that he had a neckcloth at home made of double chain lightning, and that he could never come to his full height till the clouds were lifted a piece. He called himself a west wind full of prickles, a dose for old Kaintuck and a drawing plaster for the Allegheny mountains. The fact is he war too smart to live long, and screamed himself to death, one night, to show his spirit. I knowed him when he war a boy, and seed him when he war a man, and went to his funeral when he war dead. He war the pride of the country, and could out-scream seven catamounts tied together.

Col. Crockett Beat by Mike Fink

I expect, stranger, you think old Davy Crockett war never beat at the long rifle; but he war tho. I expect there's no man so strong, but what he will find some one stronger. If you haven't heerd tell of one Mike Fink, I'll tell you something about him, for he war a helliferocious fellow, and made an almighty fine shot. Mike was a boatman on the Mississippi, but he had a little cabin on the head of the Cumberland, and a horrid handsome wife, that loved him the wickedest that ever you seen. Mike only worked enough to find his wife in rags, and himself in powder and lead and whiskey, and the rest of the time he spent in knocking over bar and turkeys, and bouncing deer, and sometimes drawing a lead on an Injun.

So one night I fell in with him in the woods, where him and his wife shook down a blanket for me in his wigwam.

In the morning sez Mike to me, "I've got the handsomest wife, and the fastest horse, and the sharpest shooting iron in all Kentuck, and if any man dare doubt it, I'll be in his hair quicker than hell could scorch a feather."

This put my dander up, and sez I, "I've nothing to say agin your wife, Mike, for it can't be denied she's a shocking hand-some woman, and Mrs. Crockett's in Tennessee, and I've got no horses. Now Mike, I don't exactly like to tell you you lie about what you say about your rifle, but I'm d----d if you speak the truth, and I'll prove it. Do you see that ar cat sitting on the top rail of your potato patch, about a hundred and fifty yards off? If she ever hears agin, I'll be shot if it shant be without ears."

So I blazed away, and I'll bet you a horse, the ball cut off both the old tom cat's ears close to his head, and shaved the hair off clean across the skull, as slick as if I'd done it with a razor, and the critter never stirred, nor knew he'd lost his ears till he tried to scratch 'em.

"Talk about your rifle after that, Mike!" sez I.

"Do you see that ar sow away off furder than the eend of the world," sez Mike, "with a litter of pigs round her?"; and he lets fly. The old sow give a grunt, but never stirred in her tracks, and Mike falls to loading and firing for dear life, till he hadn't left one of them pigs enough tail to make a toothpick on.

"Now," sez he, "Col. Crockett, I'll be pretticularly obleedged to you if you'll put them ar pig's tails on again."

"That's onpossible, Mike," sez I, "but you've left one of 'em about an inch to steer by, and if it had a-been my work, I wouldn't have done it so wasteful. I'll mend your shot"; and so I lets fly, and cuts off the apology he'd left the poor cretur for decency. I wish I may drink the whole of Old Mississip, without a drop of the real stuff in it, if you wouldn't have thort the tail had been drove in with a hammer.

That made Mike a kinder sorter wrothy, and he sends a ball after his wife as she was going to the spring after a gourd full of water, and knocked half her comb out of her head, without stirring a hair, and calls out to her to stop for me to take a bliz-zard at what was left on it. The angeliferous critter stood still as a scarecrow in a cornfield, for she'd got used to Mike's tricks by long practice.

"No, no, Mike," sez I, "Davy Crockett's hand would be sure to shake if his iron war pointed within a hundred mile of a shemale, and I give up beat, Mike. And as we've had our eye-openers a-ready, we'll now take a flem-cutter, by way of an anti-fogmatic,* and then we'll disperse."

Crockett and the Puke

I war walking along, one day, near the shore of the Massis-sippi, when I seed a Puke a short piece ahead of me. When he seed me, he grounded his rifle, and waited for me to come up. I seed that and put on more steam. "Stranger." he hollered, "can you tell me how fur it is from here to the pig-pen whar Colonel Crockett lives?"

That made me feel wolfish, you can't purtend to deny, but I hung fire and squat low, and answered him sorter civil, though I grinned like a red-hot tommyhawk. Sez I, "Davy Crockett lives about two miles from here, but his house is no pig-pen, d'ye see. I take it he has as good a house, keeps as good whiskey, and as pritty a wife, as any human."

"Stranger, you are somewhat crusty," sez he, "but I wants to git a sight of this Colonel Crockett, for I can take the rag off every thing in Old Kaintuck, and have ammunition to spare."

I turned right round and spit at him. He dodged it, and began to sharpen his thumb nail. Then I felt so mad, the trees looked all colors, and sez I, "Stranger, I'm a coming! I'm Colonel Crockett, you white-livered, green-eyed scorpion, and I'll carry home one of your eyes this day."

"Please the lord," sez he, "you won't put your corkscrew into my face. But if your name is Davy Crockett, I'll have you know that I'm a hoss what never war rode, fresh from the stables on the north side of Snapping Devil Creek, shod with steel-traps, and rubbed down with essence of thunder cloud. I'm just fed, and at ease, ready for a race or a fight, a shoot or a sail, a turn or a twist. I'm jist born in this world for a special purpose; and if you put your hand to my throat, you can feel the grit all up and down my windpipe."

*"An alcoholic beverage taken on the pretext of counteracting the effects of fog," *Dictionary of American English,* Craigie and Hulbert, eds.

34

When I heered that, I jumped rite off the ground, and ran around in a circle three times and squealed with all my might. After I had done squealing, I screamed; then I begun to holler; and, at last, I jumped up and crowed! When the Puke seed my cream had fairly riz, he put himself in a postur, and I came into his bread basket feet foremost. That wur no time for making observations. He war explunctificated, rum-squaddled, and boliterated. He clapped his hands on his bowels, and swore he war a steembote with a busted biler. I then give him my hand, and he said he'd agree to overlook it this time.

So we went home together, and when he seed my house, and tasted my whiskey, and looked at my wife, he vowed the house war a palace, the whiskey war better than brandy, and my wife war more pritty than the forest rose. As soon as we war both got well drunk, we went to bed.

My Neighbor Grizzle

Bartholomew Grizzle lived next door to me, about four miles off, for ten year. He war quite temperate at fust, and didn't drink more than three quarts of whiskey in a day; but he soon got a love for the stuff, and then he drunk all the time. What with his hard drinking, and what with having his head smashed to pieces by a tree, and what with a consumption that he had for two year, it carried him off; and I have never forgot Bartholomew to this day. When he died, a wooden monniment war put on his grave, and as they have built a tavern close to the place whar he wur berried, it sarves as a hoss-block and monniment now. They talked of carving his epitaff on the monniment; but I telled 'em that would be of no use, as he coodn't read, and he could only make his mark with a rifle, on the hide of some varmint of the forest.

The Way they Travel in the West

A Kentucky Team

Thar is some fokes that makes much of their figgers and larning and all sorts of inventions, and I spose when they got their steembotes and railrodes a-goin' they thort they war going to upset the world rite off and make the sun rise by steam, and contrive a new way to make calves grow up to be oxen in one nite; but I'll be shot if I ever wanted to use any thing better than God's critters, which he has made with legs and fins to swim.

As for your steembotes and railrode whirligigs they are only a sapling compared to what Bartholomew Grithard did last fall. I war going out with my dog Tiger to persecute some of the varmints in Little Creek near Yellow-leg Swamp, when I seed the waters of the Massissippy in a wuss pother than the Pukes at the election. I knowed it warn't a steembote bekase thar war no smoke, but the spray war thick enuff to make up for it. I run down by the side of the river to smell out the muss, and then I seed a alligator's head, and then his tail whisking about like a sapling in a whirlwind. But I seed that Bartholomew was rite arter the varmint in his boat, and he war going at sich a rate I knowed he would tree him before long. Then I seed another pesky great alligator cutting out like all possessed rite along side of the tother one. So I up with my gun to shoot, and Bartholomew bawled out to me to hold fire, for the two varmints was tackled up and harnessed to his bote, and he war driving 'em down stream. That war a settler and I stood and grinned at 'em till I loosened two of my front teeth, and as soon as they got out o' sight, I haw-hawed rite out a-laffing, and I laffed for about half an hour, so violent that the trees shed all their leaves.

A day or two arterwards, I met Bartholomew in the woods, and he told me he hoped I would be keerful not to draw a lead on any of his critters, as he had a number what he war trying to break for the harness. I asked him if he thort any christian cretur would use them pesky, unsarkumsized alligators. He said he knowed it, and then he went on to say that he had one team as war parfectly kind in harness, and that he should put

37

in all he knew to git a chance for to carry the mail with that team. He sed how he had sent an invite to Amos Kendall* to come and look at his beasts, and he should let Mister Kendall drive 'em out a few, round about the Great Bend, if he wan't satisfied without doin' on it.

Arter a while Bartholomew found it cost a pleggy sight to keep 'em, and he turned 'em out to graze, and they all cut dirt up stream and didn't come back at nite, the ongrateful critters. But Bartholomew said he shouldn't keered nothing much about it only for one young one that war jist come of age, which he war trying to break in for the saddle, so as he could go to meeting on Sunday without using his bote.

Riproarious Fight on the Mississippi River

One day as I was sitting in the starn of my broad horn, the old "Free and Easy," on the Mississippi, taking a horn of midshipman's grog, with a tin pot in each hand, first a draught of whiskey, and then one of river water, who should float down past me but Jo Snag. He was in a snooze, as fast as a church, with his mouth wide open; he had been ramsquaddled with whiskey for a fortnight, and as it evaporated from his body, it looked like the steam from a vent pipe. Knowing the feller would be darned hard to wake, with all this steam on, as he floated past me I hit him a crack over his knob with my big steering oar. He waked in a thundering rage.

Says he, "Hallo stranger, who axed you to crack my lice?"

Said I, "Shut up your mouth, or your teeth will get sunburnt."

Upon this he crooked up his neck and neighed like a stallion. I clapped my arms and crowed like a cock.

Says he, "If you are a game chicken, I'll pick all the pin feathers off of you."

*Postmaster-General, 1835-40.

For some time back I had been so wolfy about the head and shoulders, that I was obliged to keep kivered up in a salt crib to keep from spiling; for I had not had a fight for as much as ten days. So says I, "Give us none of your chin music, but set your kickers on land, and I'll give you a severe licking."

The fellow now jumped ashore, and he was so tall he could not tell when his feet were cold. He jumped up on a rod.

Says he, "Take care how I light on you"; and he gave me a real sockdologer that made my very liver and lights turn to jelly.

But he found me a real scrouger. I brake three of his ribs, and he knocked out five of my teeth and one eye. He was the severest colt that ever I tried to break. I finally got a bite hold of his posteriors, that he could not shake off. We were now parted by some boatmen, and we were so exorsted that it was more than a month before either could have a fight. It seemed to me like a little eternity. And although I didn't come out second best, I took care not to wake up a ring-tailed roarer with an oar again.

A Hard Head

An old gentleman was relating a story of one of your "half horse, half alligator" Mississippi boatmen. Says he: "He is a hard head, for he stood under an oak tree in a thunder storm, when the lightning struck the tree, and he dodged it several times, when finding he could not dodge it any longer, he stood and took nine claps in succession on his head and never flinched."

Lodging
in Kansas

I tell you what, stranger, I have gone in for a great majority of different sorts o' lodging an' sleeping, in the course o' my travels. I have slept alongside o' a log, and peeled off the bark for a coverlid; I've slept on a big rock with the snow for a blanket; I've roosted up a tree with a wildcat for a pillow; but the style of lodging in Kansas Territory beats all that clean out o' creation. You see, you can't lie upon a board or plank, because there ain't any there; you can't lie on the ground, because it is covered with water; you can't lie on the old rocks, because they're covered with rattlesnakes: so the only way left to get yourself into the snoreifferous state is to hook your two arms on to the lower limbs of a tree, with the ground and water for a foot-bard, an' there, like a man upon the gallows, you can swing yourself into a gentle slumber, keep off the snakes an' red-skins, and no one can say that you ain't getting your lodging in an upright manner. This is a downright fact; if it ain't, take my narves for telegraph-wires!

A Wisconsin Squatter

May I be tetotaciously exflunctificated if I ain't off for Ouchmouchwouchio, Rattlesnake county, Wisconsin Territory; and may I be turned into a York dandy, if I don't squat on the fattest prarie in them 'are parts. I'm a wild cat wolf breed, can skin a crocodile in two minutes, and draw it on an alligator, in half that time. I'll beat the greatest whirlwind you can turn out, and gin him ten oak trees and a hickory sapling start. I'm a copperheaded screamer, and my mama's a worser. I've got a petrified mammoth for my young 'uns to play with, and maybe he ain't a beauty. Next year I'll tell you how I cotch'd him.

Hands of Celebrated Gougers

It's got everlastin fashionable, now-a-days, since the Doghairy-o-type* machine has come into use, for every created critter, from a man to a cart and horse, to have the likenesses of their heads; but I go in for the hands, and I here give you correct portraits of the hands of three of the greatest and most skintearifferous gougers that were ever known in or outside of earthly geography. They are the true nat'ral gouging instruments.

No. 1 is the fin of the ferocious Mike Fink, the great Alligator

*Daguerreotype.

41

Gouger. Now that ar paw war a parfect explosion to all that nasty scaly crawling race of mortal critters. He used to gouge thar eyes an' tongues out first, an' then punch thar bodies out of thar shells as handsome as a kernel out of a nut; he made a flatboat of alligator hides that has been running up and down the Big Muddy a leetle before and ever since.

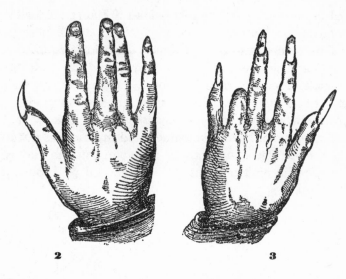

2   3

No. 2 is the paw of Capt. Stackpole, the gum gouger, that war of the true harrow tooth disposition, for he could take an injun's scalp in the natural way; that is, he had jist to make a mark in the critter's skull with that ar thumb nale, and the whole skin would peel off clar to the bone as slick as an injun.

No. 3 is the great claw of Ralph Nimrod, the wildcat gouger; his nails war a kind of natural spring steel; they stuck out about a feet, and in gouging they stuck in about a feet and a half, and they generally met each other on the outside, and their sharp points grinned at you like a row of sharks teeth in a shoal.

Crockett Delivering His Celebrated War Speech

"Fellow Citizens and Humans:

"These is times that come upon us like a whirlwind, and an airthquake: they are come like a catamount on the full jump! We are called upon to show our grit like a chain lightning agin a pine log, to extarminate, mollify, and calumniate the foe like a niggar put into a holler log and rammed down with a young sapling!

"Pierce the heart of the enemy as you would a feller that spit

43

in your face, knocked down your wife, burnt up your houses, and called your dog a skunk! Cram his pesky carcass full of thunder and lightning like a stuffed sassidge and turtle him off with a red hot poker, so that there won't be a piece of him left big enough to give a crow a breakfast, and bite his nose off into the bargain. Split his countenance with a live airthquake, and tarrify him with a rale Injun yell, till he gives up all his pertensions to the clearings this side of Salt Pond, and clears out like a streak of greased lightning chased by the crocodiles of the Mississippi.

"Hosses, I am with you! and while the stars of Uncle Sam, and the stripes of his country wave triumphantly in the breeze, whar, whar, whar is the craven, low-lived, chicken-bred, toad-hoppin', red-mounted, bristle-headed mother's son of ye who will not raise the beacon light of triumph, smouse the citadel of the aggressor, and squeeze ahead for Liberty and Glory! Whoop! h-u-rah, hosses, come along — Crockett's with you — show us the enemy!"

Receipt for a Cold

The following reseat from my great aunt will be useful for the reader, and he'd better tend to it. When you find you have got a cold, go into the forest and find out a young painter that's about two years old. Chase him till you catch him; and then take off his hide, and lay it warm upon your bowels. Drink two pints of whiskey, and go to sleep. You may git up in the course of the night five or six times and scream. If that don't cure you, then you may say Davy Crockett never went to Congress, that's all.

DOUGHTY DAMES

The Flower of Gum Swamp

The flower of Gum Swamp war a gal by the name of Lotty Ritchers. She stood six foot in her shoes; but as she hadn't 'em on very often, she war not quite so high. She used to brag that she war a streak of litenin set up edgeways, and buttered with quicksilver. She chased a crockodile one evening till his hide come off, and one day I met her in the forest jist as she had killed a monstracious big bear. I seed it war too much for her great strength, so we laid holt together; she took the tail, and I the head part, and for this she treated me to a slice of genuine

steak. She still wears the shift that she made out of the varmint's skin. It is told on her that she carried twenty eyes in her work bag, at one time, that she had picked out of the heads of certain gals of her acquaintance. She always made them into a string of beads, when she went to church, and wore 'em round her neck. She never pared her nails, and had holes cut in her shoes, so that her toe nails could have room to grow. She war a real

47

beauty; but the young fellers war shy of her, bekase she never could kort long before she wanted to box with her bo, and her thumb nail war great for pulling out eyes. Finely she cotch'd her death by standing two days up to her chin in the Massissippy to hail the steembotes as they past by.

Colonel Coon's Wife Judy

It's most likely my readers has all heered of Colonel Coon's wife Judy. She wore a bearskin petticoat, an alligator's hide for an over-coat, an eagle's nest for a hat, with a wild-cat's tail for a feather. When she was fourteen years old, she wrung off a snapping turtle's neck and made a comb of its shell, which she wears to this day. When she was sixteen years old, she run down a four year old colt, and chased a bear three mile through the snow, because she wanted his hair to make a tooth brush. She out-screamed a catamount, on a wager, when she was just come of age; and sucked forty rattlesnakes' eggs to give her a sweet breath, the night she was married.

It was not at all likely that Judy would throw herself away on any young feller that was a mind to set up a claim to her, and so many of 'em found they were barking up the wrong tree and getting their fingers pricked with a chestnut burr. At last, one Tennessee roarer, that never backed out for any thing short of a mammoth, heard of Judy's accomplishments, and 'tarmined to try his flint agin her steel. So he got into a jumper on a cold winter night, and drove through the woods towards her father's house. He begun to scream before he got within sight of the log hut where Judy lived, and his voice was heard five mile off. Judy's heart begun to beat when she heard him, for she knew whoever he was, he was a whole steamboat. When he got to the house, he give one leap from his jumper, dashed down the door, and bounced into the middle of the room.

"Tom Coon, by G—d!" cried every one in the house — for he was no stranger by fame, though they had never seen him before. Judy right away set down in a corner of the room to try his spunk, and said not a word, good or bad. He pulled half a dozen eyes out of his pocket, and flinging 'em down on the floor, swore with a round oath he'd place any man's eyes by the side of them that dared to say a word agin Judy!

Judy then jumped up like a frog and said, "Tom Coon, I'm yours for life — I know what you've come for, and I'll be your wedded wife without any more fustification about it."

So Tom got Judy and all her plunder. Tom took her into Tennessee with him right away, and begun to make a little clearing in the midst of the wood.

Judy soon gave him a speciment of her talents. For, being out one evening to a tea-squall, about ten mile off, in coming home through the wood she found a nest of young wild-cats in the stump of a tree. She said nothing about it when she went home, but let her toe-nails grow till they were an inch long. Then she started all alone, one morning, and went to the nest, and, jumping in upon the young wild-cats, stamped them to death with her feet. It was quite a tough job, and they bit her legs most ridiculously; but she stood up to the mark, though they scratched her backsides so tarnaciously they've never itched since.

Sal Fink, the Mississippi Screamer

I dare say you've all on you, if not more, frequently heard this or that great she-human crittur boasted of, an' pointed out as "one o' the gals"— but I tell you what, stranger, you have never really set your eyes on "one o' the gals" till you have seen Sal Fink, the Mississippi screamer.

She fought a duel once with a thunderbolt, an' came off without a singe, while at the fust fire she split the thunderbolt all to flinders, an' gave the pieces to Uncle Sam's artillerymen to touch off their cannon with. When a gal about six years old, she used to play see-saw on the Mississippi snags, and arter she war done she would snap 'em off, an' so cleared a large district of the river. She used to ride down the river on an alligator's back, standing upright, an' dancing "Yankee Doodle," and could leave all the steamers behind. But the greatest feat she ever did, positively outdid anything that ever was did.

One day when she war out in the forest, making a collection o' wildcat skins for her family's winter bedding, she war captered in the most all-sneakin' manner by about fifty Injuns, an' carried by 'em to Roastflesh Hollow, whar the blood-drinkin' wild varmints determined to skin her alive, sprinkle a leetle salt over her, an' devour her before her own eyes. So they took an' tied her to a tree, to keep till mornin' should bring the rest o' thar ring-nosed sarpints to enjoy the fun. Arter that, they lit a large fire in the holler, turned the bottom o' thar feet towards the blaze, Injun fashion, and went to sleep to dream o' thar mornin's feast. Well, arter the critturs got into a somniferous snore, Sal got into an all-lightnin' of a temper, and burst all the ropes about her like an apron string. She then found a pile o' ropes, took and tied all the Injun's heels together all around the fire; then fixin' a cord to the shins of every two couple, she, with a suddenachous jerk, that made the entire woods tremble, pulled the entire lot o' sleepin' red-skins into that ar great fire, fast together — an' then sloped* like a panther out of her pen, in the midst o' the tallest yellin', howlin', scramblin' and singin', that war ever seen or heerd on, since the great burnin' o' Buffalo prairie!

Nance Bowers Taming a Bear

Nance Bowers, the youngest daughter of my sister Aggy, war about as fair a sample of full grown female flesh as ever flourished outside of the garden of Eden. She war seven feet tall, out of her stockings and hair comb. She could outscream a thunderbolt or a dozen wildcats, wipe her feet with her hair, swing on the top of a fifty foot hickory tree, and eat more wildcat steaks raw than any other livin' critter in creation. She had one of the most universally useful mouths in her face

*Left hastily.

50

that ever fell to the head of humanity; she could eat victuals
with one corner, whistle with the other, and scream with the
middle; she could grin with her upper lip, and frown all sorts
of temptation with the under one. She could scratch the skin
off of an alligator with her toe-nail, and snap a ten foot sarpint's head off by a single gal-vanic jerk of his tail.

I'll never forget the trick of her using up, and civilizin' the
great king bear of Mud Forest. You see, the great critter took
it into his head, one day, to walk into her smoke house, an' fodder himself upon a smoked ham or two. Then nat'rally growin'

more impudent, he walked into her kitchen, an' grabbed her
around the bosom, thinking to squeeze the gizzard out of her
before she could say who or boo.

But I tell you what, the bear-faced varmint war taken by
surprise, for she had jist taken hot dumplings out of the pot,
for dinner, an' she turned her head suddenaciously round,
smacked a big red hot smoking one into the critter's throat,
and the way it made his eyes wink boilin' water, war a caution to a high pressure steamboat boiler. Arter that, she took
an' grabbed him by the tail, and licked him till he shed

enough bear's grease through his hide to supply twenty-seven perfume shops; and the critter became so docile and domestic, that he sarves, to this day, both for dog and horse. He tends to all her cows an' niggers, supplies her with bear's oil for her family, lends her his paws for tongs, ovens, rakes, grid-iron an' hoes; and when she wants to cross Big Muddy River, he takes her in his paws, as a nurse takes a baby, and carries her across as upright as a Yankee soldier, and brings her on shore, as dry as a smoking fire poker.

Katy Goodgrit and the Wolves

Katy Goodgrit war a favorite of mine, bekase when her spunk war up, she could grin a wildcat out of countenance, and make a streak of lightning back out. She didn't care for anything that went on four legs, nor anything that went on two legs. One day she war going out into the woods, and seed two wolves shying along like a snake in the grass, not a great ways off; and she intarmined to put a stop to 'em, for they looked very obnoxious, and seemed to want to be tasting sumthing of the human kind. So she took up a club, and walked in between 'em. They begun to feel amazing skittish when they seed her coming with the club, but at last they come towards her. She gave one of 'em a monstracious tap on the head with her club, and he squawked right out. Before she had time to hit the other, she heerd a pattering amongst the leaves, and when she lookt around, thar war about fifty wolves coming towards her on the full trot.

Some gals would have ben skeered out of thar seven wits, but Katy always knowed it war the fust duty of a gal of Kaintuck to stand up to her lick log, salt or no salt. So she just squatted low for the present, and got up into a holler stump whar the wolves couldn't quite reach her, and they come roaring around her, like the water boiling around Crocodile Rock, at Tumble Down Falls. They jump up evenmost to her face, and she spit at one so violent that it knocked his

52

eye out. She cotch another by the scurf of his neck, and whipt his head off agin the tree. So she kept stopping their wind, till the fust she knew thar war a pile of dead wolves around the tree, high enough for the others to climb up on it. Then she war obleeged to squat down, or they would have tore her head off.

She staid thar all nite; but early the nixt morning she stuck up her head, and crowed, till she crowed and screamed all the wolves deaf, and then they begun to clear out, but she went arter 'em with a pole and killed half of 'em before they got away.

Sappina Wing and the Crocodile

The biggest thing that ever happent in our cleering war the time that Oak Wing's darter Sappina war mopping up the floor one day. She war all alone in the house as her mother had gone to a tea-squall and had took a tame wolf with her; for it war one that she had cotch an' tamed, an' she loved it as she did her own child. Her mother had agreed to scream as soon as she got down to Gander Creek, which is about three mile from the house. Sappina heered a scream but she couldn't rightly tell whether it war her mother or a catamount as the voices of the two war alike. At last she heered something rubbing an' scratching along the side of the house, an' she turned towards the door an' seed a big crocodile crawling right in at the door. She backed up in one corner till he got in, an' opened his mouth as if he would ax her to walk into a ball room. Then her dander riz, an' she lifted the mop an' pointed rite at his infarnal tongue, an' rammed it down his throat. He struggled about five minnits most beautiful, an' broke all the crockery with his tail, but his breathing hole was stopt up, an' the cretur died.

A Bear Skinned

One day when Oak Wing's sister war going to a baptizing, and had her feed in a bag under her arm, she seed a big bear that had come out from a holler tree, and he looked first at her, then at the feed, as if he didn't know which to eat fust.

He kinder poked out his nose, and smelt of the dinner, which war sassengers made of bear's meat and crocodile's liver. She stood a minute and looked at him, in hopes he would feel ashamed of himself and go off; but he then come up and smelt of her, and so she thort twar time to be stirring. So she threw the dinner down before him, an' when he put his nose to it, to take a bite, she threw herself on him, an' caught the scuff of his neck in her teeth; an' the bear shot ahead, for it felt beautiful, as her teeth war as long and as sharp as nails. He tried to run, an' she held on with her teeth, an' it stript the skin clear off of him, and left him as naked as he was born; she held on with her teeth till it come clear off the tail. The bear was seen a week arterwards up in Muskrat Hollow, running without his skin. She made herself a good warm petticoat out of the pesky varmint's hide.

A Poundiferous Gal

Sal Fungus war one of the most poundiferous gals in old Alligator Clearing, which lies between Roaring River and Dead Man's Holler. Once I war going out to take a little walk in the morning, about ten or fifteen minutes into the forest, and breathe the fresh air, when I heard a pesky rustling and thrashing amongst the dry leaves and bushes. I cut down to the place whar the voice come from, and I seed Sal Fungus thar, and a big injun. Sal kicked his fundaments, and he slapt her face; then she wrung his nose till the blood spurted, and that war what made him so mad.

Well, arter that my attachment for Sal grew taller and wider every day, and we courted, hunted and walked together night and day. Bime by, she could scalp an Injun, skin a bear, grin down hickory nuts, laugh the bark off a pine tree, swim stark up a cataract, gouge out alligator's eyes, dance a rock to pieces, sink a steamboat, blow out the moonlight, tar and feather a Puke, ride a painter bare-back, sing a wolf to sleep and scratch his hide off. But her heart growed too big; and when I left her to go to Texas, it burst like an airthquake, and poor Sal died. She died with a bursted heart — it war too big with love for me, and it's case war not big enough to hold it. She war buried with the honors o' war. I used to go every nite for a week arterwards and fire a salute of a hundred guns over her grave to show my respect for so much true grit. A week arter that I went to Texas.

Crockett Popping the Question

Every human in our clearing always thought it war thar duty to take a vartuous gal, and replenish the airth, especially in our parts o' the world, whar folks war pesky scarce, and the painters and bears war ennermost all the population, speckled with crocodiles and rattlesnakes. Thar war a gal that lived a smart piece from my cabin that I had seed flog two bears, for eatin up her under petticoat; an' every blow she hit 'em, war a Cupid's arrow goin' into my gizzard. So I put on my best raccoon skin cap and sallied out to see her.

When I got within three miles of her house I began to scream, till you could see my voice a-goin' through the air like flashes of lightning on a thunder-bolt — it sounded most beautiful to her, for it went through the woods like a harrycane, and I warn't far behind it. When she heered it pretty nigh, she come out, and climbed up the biggest tree thar; and when she reached the top, she took off her barr skin petticoat, the one she died red with tiger's blood, the day her mother kicked the bucket; and then she tied it fast to a big limb, and waved it most splendiferous. I soon came up to her, and she made one jump down to meet me. I cotch'd her in my arms, and gin her such a hug that her tung stuck out half a foot, and then we kissed about half an hour, and arter that I popped the question. She 'greed to have me if I'd promise to have no babies; but she let me off from that agreement pesky quick arter we war tied together.

BEN HARDING

The Early Days, Love and Courtship of Ben Harding

(Member of Congress from Kentucky, as related to Col. Crockett by himself.)

BEN HARDING AT SCHOOL

As the public seems to be very anxious to hear all about my friend Colonel Crockett, I don't see no reason why I should not make some stir in the world, too, as we are both members of Congress. I have long had an intention to write my life, and tell about the wild varmints that I have killed, and how I got to be elected member of Congress, and all that.

I was born in Kentucky and there's where I was reared. I knowed how to handle a rifle before I was five years old, and gouged out four eyes before I was sixteen. I bit off a fellow's nose on the same day that I come of age, and waded a river when I was twenty-five. When I was about twelve years old, my parents sent me to school. It was none of my seeking, for I could never see any use in larning. A man can kill an alligator without larning; he can tree a bear without larning; and he can lick his enemy without larning — so that a great deal of time is thrown away by going to school, when a boy might be employing his time to better purpose.

Well, the schoolmaster was a young flirt that had got his eddycation in some big city, and then cut out to the backwoods to make his fortin by keeping school. He went all round to the parents of the children to ax them for their custom, and the old folks was mighty glad to get him, but the boys looked at him like he had been a wild varmint, for they knowed he would keep 'em in the house when they wanted to go out of doors a-hunting. So me and two other boys set out to go to his school though we didn't mean to take any of his lip, for ary one of us could double up two such fellows any minute. But we packed off to please the old folks.

59

The school house was a little log house not more than twelve foot square, by the side of a large clearing. We went in and found about forty boys there, and ten gals. All the boys had brought their rifles and butcher knives with them, so that if they got a chance to take a blizzard at any thing on the way, they might improve the time. We all set down on the benches, and the master began to ax us all round about our knowledge in larning, and when we told him we did not know our letters, he looked at us as spiteful as if we had been bear's cubs, and said we was as ignorant as savages. We looked rather striped at this, for every one in our parts hated the savages as we did pison. But we didn't make any answer, for we wanted to see how fur he would go for to provoke us.

He then began to range us into classes, but in the midst of it all, one of the big boys got to carrying on most uproariously with a big gal, and the master called him up, and took a ruler and told him to hold out his hand — so he didn't know what the master was a-going to do with his hand, and he held it out, and then the master gave him a whack over the hand with his ruler. With that the boy tackled to him; "root hog or die," was the word, and the master came to the floor, all the gals cleared out, and away they went over the hills like a herd of young buffaloes, and the small boys followed them. I cut for home like a cane-brake on fire, but presently the master was seen coming, running like a heavy thaw, after us. He had a stick in one hand, and we didn't care to wait for him. So that was the last of his school-keeping in them parts.

SCRAPES IN THE BACKWOODS

Well, I staid about home after this, sometimes setting traps for wild-cats, and sometimes shooting bears and deer. At last the war broke out, and then I marched under General Jackson against the English at New Orleens. When we was about starting for New Orleens, I composed the celebrated song, well known to every backwoodsman, and which was wonderfully admired at the time, beginning with,

"Come all you bold Kentuckians, I'd have you all to know
That for to fight the enemy, we're going for to go."

I believe it was this song that did more than any thing else towards getting me to Congress, for when it was seen that I had talents, I grew very popular all at once.

Before I went home from the wars, I met a big fellow on the levee at New Orleans, who thought to take advantage of my youth, and begun blackguarding me about my countrymen, for he didn't belong to Kentucky himself.

Says he, "You call yourselves half horse and half alligator, but I'll let you know that I'm whole alligator with a cross of the wildcat."

I jumped up and snapped my fingers in his face, and told him that I didn't care the fag end of a johnny cake for him, and I spit right in his mouth. With that he came at me with his mouth wide open; he just missed my ear, and I snapped at his nose and seized it between my teeth. He roared and struggled but I held on like a pair of pinchers, until at last off came his nose.

"That's into you," says I, "for an alligator — you see I'm crossed with the snapping turtle!"

Well, I went home once more, and found every thing pretty much as I left it, and fell to hunting bears right away. In one season I killed twenty-five bears, besides two wildcats and a possum. I was out one day and got benighted, when I laid down to sleep by the side of a river. I laid my head on a great log, and closed my eyes. I hadn't been long asleep before the log began to move, and I jumped on my feet, when what should the log be but a great crocodile. He raised his head and opened his pesky great mouth to bite me in two. I jumped right down his throat. He whisked about and thrashed up the ground like an earthquake for a few minutes, but presently he give over, complete choked to death, and I found hard work to get out again.

BEN GOES A-COURTING

Crockett Takes Up the Story

Having come to the years of maturity, and being a stout lad of his age, young Harding began to look around for a wife. Having heard of one Betsey Buzzard, a good stout gal, not very high, but making up what she wanted in longness by being pretty thick through, and as round as an apple, he cut out for the house where she lived. Ben considered himself a whole team, and went about trapping this gal just as he would tree a bear.

He felt pretty queer when he had got near the house where she lived, and had a good mind to turn back and not go in, as he was afeard she would have nothing to say to him. But he knowed that "faint heart never won fair lady," and so he stood still awhile to wait till his courage got up; but he found the longer he stood, the more his courage went away, and he began to fear if he stood much longer, he should not dare to go at all. So he thought he would take only one long step towards the house, as there couldn't be any thing decisive in that. Then he took another step, and so on until he had only one step to take to the house, and now he found that that last step was just as much as if he hadn't taken any steps before, for he was puzzled just as much how to go ahead as he was before he stopped at all. The way his heart bobbed up and down was a caution. He dassent so much as look over his shoulder, and much less look ahead; he was stuck in the mud like a Mississippi sawyer, and thought he would rather face a whole regiment of wildcats than look Betsey in the face, but 'twasn't because he didn't love her, only 'twas a dubus thing to make the first attempt, and not know nothing about how he would be received.

Just then the door opened, and Betsey herself come out all rigged up in her best bib and tucker, and Ben was dumb-foundered right away, and his heart came up into his throat, specially as Betsey was cross-eyed, and he thought she was looking right at him, whereas she was looking towards the hovel where the horses was kept. There she stood right on the door stone, and

Ben felt it would be impossible for him to speak to her, but pretty soon another fellow come out of the barn, leading along a horse towards Betsey. Then Ben forgot his bashfulness all at once, and his dander riz right up.

"I say, stranger," said he, "do you make purtentions to this gal?"

The fellow let go the horse and looked right at Ben, as if he would eat him up alive! Ben knew what would come next very well, and sure enough the other fellow made a dive at one of his eyes, but Ben jumped up his whole length and lit right on the other feller's head. Both of them tumbled together against an old gate, leading into a watermillion patch, and the way the vines was snarled about their legs and the way the watermillions got squished was a caution. Sometimes he was uppermost and sometimes the tother, until at last Betsey, who had taken a notion to Ben, jumped astraddle of the other feller's back when he was down, and began pounding him with a stone over the head. When he seed that, he give over right away, for it went so to his heart that his gal should turn agin him that he couldn't fight. He got on his feet and shook himself, and he turned all colors when he seed Ben go right up to Betsey and give her a smack on the cheek.

Says Ben to himself, "Mister, I think you are most catawampiously chawed up!" The feller said not a word but turned his tail and went straight off, and was never heered on arterwards.

BEAR SCRAPE AT A CAMP MEETING

The gal then told Ben that she had been a going to set out with that feller for camp meeting, and that if he liked, he might take his place on the horse. So Ben got right up on the horse, and took Betsey up behind him, and they drove off to camp meeting, at the distance of about ten miles. On the road they courted with all their might, till Ben got her to agree to have him, though she little thought, all that time, that he would one day be a member of Congress. When they reached the camp, they found the preachers all very earnestly engaged,

63

some a-praying, and some a-preaching and some a-singing sams. There was one feller in perticular that hollored so you could hear him as far as a catamount, and he stamped worse than a fulling mill. There was guards placed all round to prevent the gals runing after the fellers. There was a great many tents where the ministers penned up the gals to convert them; and some on 'em was hollerin like they were going mad.

At last one minister come along and asked Ben and Betsey to be converted — so he got up on the trunk of a tree to preach them a sarment, when, just in the middle of it, he slumped in, for it was a holler tree, and he sunk clean down out of sight; but he was so arnest, that he kept on preaching in the tree, till a great bear that was inside with him woke up and begun to move, when he hollered out that the devil was gouging him most ridiculous. Then Betsey laughed right out for she knowed it was a bear; and she climbed up the tree, so as to lower down a rope to him and help him out. Finally, somehow or somehow else, they got the minister out of the holler tree, and he said he had been swallored up in a whale like Jonah. But presently the bear come breaching from the tree like a steamboat. Then such a scratching and hollering as there was you never see. They thought the devil had broke loose upon them sure enough. They upset the tents in their hurry to cut out, and there was one minister that was so fat he couldn't run very fast, and the bear gained upon him every step he took, when Betsey walked right up to him and stuck him with a knife.

Howsomever there was no more praying or preaching that day, and as Ben and Betsey had a great deal of courting to go through with they cut out for home. Ben had some curious talk with the gal, on the way home, but she told him he had better wait till they were married, and so he did which happened on the very next week.

Adventure with a Tar

MEETING OF HARDING AND CROCKETT

I was laying asleep on the Mississippi one day, with a piece of river scum for a pillow, and floating down stream in rale free and easy style, when all at once I was waked up by something that come agin my ribs like it was trying to feel for an opening into my bowels. So I just raised my head to see what kind of a varmint was sharpening his teeth agin my ribs, and seed it was something that lookt so much like a human cretur that I was half a mind to speek to it. But it had a tail to its head about as big around as my arm and as long as a hoss pistle. The cretur was floating on three kegs fastened to a log, and held a pole in his hand that he had punched me with in the ribs, when I fust woke up. His trowsers was made of white sail cloth, and they was so wide about the legs that I knowed he had stoled 'em from some big fat feller, for they didn't fit him no more than my wife's raccoon skin shift would fit the fine ladies in Washington. He had on light thin shoes with big ribbons in 'em, and a painted hat with another big ribbon in that. So then I concluded rite off he had ben robbing a Yankee pedlar and got away all his flashy trumpery.

Says I, "Stranger, I take it you are a human by the looks of your face, but you are one of the greatest curiosities I've seen in these parts. I don't wonder you wake me up to look at ye."

"By the devil!" says he, "the thing has got the use of lingo like a Christian. I thought I had spoke a cat-fish. Where are you cruising, old rusty bottom? You are the queerest rigged sea craft that I ever saw, on soundings or off."

"You infarnal heathen," says I, "I don't understand all your stuff, and I spose you are fresh down this way. But I'll have you understand that I'm a snorter by birth and eddycation, and if you don't go floating along, and leave me to finish my nap I'll give you a taste of my breed. I'll begin with the snapping turtle, and after I've chawed you up with that, I'll rub you down with a spice of the alligator."

With that he looked as mad as a shovel full of hot coals, and he took a long string of tobakkur out of his pocket, and arter he had bit off a piece long enough to hang a buffalo, he roared out, "I'll shiver your mizen in less time than you can say Jack Robinson, you fresh water lubber! You rock crab! You deck sweeper! Swab!"

Says I then, for my steam begun to get rather obstropolous, "I'll double you up like a spare shirt. My name is Crockett and I'll put my mark on your infarnal wolf-hide before you've gone the length of a panther's tail further."

With that he roared right out a laffing, and I was so astonished, I held my breath to see the cretur laff on the eve of a battle. But I soon seed the reason of it, for he stooped down and reached out his hand, and says, "Tell me for God's sake, old fogy, are you the feller that makes them allmynacks about cruising after panthers and snakes and swimming over the Mississippi?"

Says I, "I'm a roarer at that bizness that you've mentioned, stranger. Going to Congress and making allmynacks is my trade!"

"Give us your flipper then, old chap," says he, "I woodn't hurt a hair of your head for the world. Isn't there a grog shop here on the coast, for by G----d I'll treat you if I sell my jacket. Hurra! three cheers for old Crockett! I'd give two weeks allowance if our boson was here; he used to read your allmynack to us on the forecastle, for, d'ye see, I can't read. I got my larning under the lee of the long boat, and swear my prayers at a lee earing in a gale o' wind. But I can read pikturs to d----n, and I could spell out your crocodile's tails from their heads when I see 'em drawed out in your book."

Beginning of a Friendship

I felt as good natured as a soaped eel when he praised up my book in this way, and I axed him how fur he was going. He said he was going to New Orleens; and then I telled him if he would come to my house, I would give him a bear steak as quick as we got there, and as much whiskey as he could put into his skin.

With that he pulled off his hat and swung it round his head

66

like he was going to fly, and he says "Come aboard, old Neptune, and I'll see your passage paid, or throw us a line and I'll give you a tow."

But I swimmed ashore, and then we went up together through the forest as good friends as a tame hawk and blind rooster. The way he walked was a caution, for he swung about like a bear skin hung to the limb of a tree. When we got home my wife didn't know what to think on him, but my darters took a mighty shine to him, and he ketched hold of Nab and gave her such a smack on the lips that she couldn't breathe for about two minnits. He said she was a slick craft, and we didn't know what that meant, but Nab said arterwards it meant that she was as sweet as honey. So we got dinner ready, and he pulled out his jacknife and the way the vittles went into him was like turning a hoss into a stable. Arter we got through, he filled a horn chock full of whiskey and didn't stop to swallow it, but it run into him jest as nat'ral as if he war born so. Then I give him a critter's head to set on, and he smoked a short pipe while I axed him about where he come from and who he was, and what was going on in Congress. He said his name was Ben Harding, and then he told such stories about what he had seed as made the gals dream o' nights for a fortnite arter he was gone; and as I spose the reader would like to hear some of 'em, I think I shall put 'em in print. He had a voice that was so ruff, I can't rite it down, but have had a cut made to pictur it out.

A Land Cruise

Talkin' of hoss-flesh one day with Ben Harding, he told me of his doins off in forrin countrys:—

"The animal I called a hoss, Kurnill Krockitt, never took my fancy exactly, for I wunst tried one. He knowed nothing about the rules of sailing, and for that I don't think thar is a cretur upon arth that is cut out for a real marine like a hoss.

"When I was in Spain where they don't go two fathum from the house without riding on a hoss, I thort I wood jest take a

turn with one, for the sake of being in the fashun. So I and a shipmate named Tom Fiferail went to a feller that had hosses layin' in dock, and axed him what he would charge to let us charter one of his hosses for the day. He told us that we could have one for six rials;* so we agreed to it, and swore we wood go aboard directly; then he fell to riggin the craft. In the fust place he put on a couple of braces, and each end of 'em led to the cretur's cutwater. Them was for to steer by, and he said they

*About 25¢ in Moroccan money.

would turn the hoss's head in a jiffy. Then he clapped a poop deck made of lether rite on the beast about midships, and lether straps hung down to put your feet in. This place was rigged up for the steersman. So Tom and I disputed which of us should take his first trick at the hellum. Tom got on and I jumped up behind; he tried to steer, but it come awkward to him to pull the wheel ropes facing the hellum, but as my back was towards the head, I could do it to a charm. So I took the braces, and Tom kept a look out ahead for breakers with his spy-glass. I found it plaguy easy steering, but the craft wouldn't mind the hellum. He went his own way, and so I had no trubble.

"At last, we hove in sight of a shantee, where was a plenty of brandy and wine, and I axed Tom if we hadn't better heave to. He agreed to it, but then we didn't know how it was done. There was a great cloth netting over the poop-deck and I thort if we could git that up, we might throw all aback, but we sot on it, and when I tried to pull it out, we both took a lurch and come near going overboard. We seed we were going on in a heavy sea-way, and was leaving the shantee astern.

"Says I, 'Tom this won't do.'

" 'Well,' says Tom, 'bring her head to the wind, and get starn-way on her.'

"So I pulled on the weather-brace and Tom took hold and helped me, and at last we got the cretur's head in the wind's eye, but she fell off on tother tack and come about; so that our heads were now towards the shantee, and then we cracked on, at the rate of ten knots. But when we got up abreast the shantee, we couldent come to a stand, but went right by it. Then we hauled on the weather brace again and away we went as far the other way till we come to a fence, and there we brought up all stand-ing. I got off, and passed Tom up a big stone, and he seized it to the end of a piece of strong three-yard spun-yarn. So I got on agin and held the stone, which was our anchor, in my lap. Then we turned the head of our craft towards the shantee, and cracked on all she could carry. As soon as we got abreast the shantee, we hauled on the weather brace and brought the head of our craft to the wind. Tom give the word—'Let go the anchor!' and I rolled the stone off the hoss's tail. But he kept on faster than ever, and as the cable was made fast around my body, I went off the horse quicker than you could say Jack Robinson.

"I jumped up and seed poor Tom going off at the rate of sixteen knots, while the craft was pitching up and down, like a brig's jibboom in a calm. Tom didn't know how to bring to, but he laid flat down, and put his arms around the hoss's neck, and held on like death to a dead nigger. At last he got hold of the long hair with his teeth and stuck like a louse in a beggar's cap. The hoss never stopt till he got to his owner's door —and I guess Tom won't try land sarvice agin."

Ben Hardin's First Fight
with a Varmint

My cousin and croney, Ben Hardin, war very savagerous at climbin' a ship's mast, an' treein' a squall; he could catch a whale by the throat, an' squeeze or flog several casks of oil out of him, if not more. But when it come to walkin' up the tall masts of the backwoods, he war like a suckin' colt in a cow stable, turnin' every way but the right way, and gettin' out no way; and the sport it used to gin me to nitiate him into the art an mystery of mesmerisin' the wild wood creatures, war enough to draw tears of fun from the eyes of a tiger.

You see, one mornin, Ben wanted me to go out in the wild-cat swamp to flog somethin to death for dinner. Out we went, an' away went Ben, whistlin' and swingin' his tarry cap at every little critter that happened to be in sight. At last we got under a venerable oak, famous for breeding so many generations of wildcats that its very knot holes looked like cat's eyes, and the limbs began to grow hairy. Well, just as we got under it, an' war goin to take a seat upon the root, we heard something gin a scratch and grunt above us, and up run Ben as light as a monkey up a ship's ladder—but he hadn't got furder than heels out of sight, before I heered a snarl, then a growl, and

70

then a sailor's reglar rough "Damn," with all the nautical trimmins. I looked up, and the critter had grabbed Ben by the
right ear, an the way the old sea-sarpint poked out his eyes
with his fists, war a caution. Down they come to the ground,
and I seed the leaves war turnin claret color. I jist stepped up
an' squeezed the life out of the critter, and give Ben a buss out
of the lightnin' bottle; he danced a jig, and swore that every
claw of the critter war a harpoon tipped with lightnin'.

Ben Hardin and Old Coppersides

"Shiver my hulk, old coppersides, but you are fallen and sinkin'
fast; keel over here, and let me pump you; why, damme, you're
capsized from want of ballast; what a pity to go down with
such a cargo of good spirits to treat the grampuses and
fishes; there, now, steady! pump away, and you'll soon right!
pump away, or swivel me, if I don't flog the grog out of
you! you etarnal ugly copper-bound land shark! Why you

71

ugly red swab, you never knowed what a great commander Captain Grog is; he's the master of storm and danger, an' will never sink a man unless he turns pirate and takes more than his just allowance! Why colt me, if ever your long-knife crew knowed how good the great father was, till you passed some o' the freight o' that ar jug down your scupper! That's the liquor to larn you savage cannibals human nater; an' the missionary Captains always gives it too, when they'd be sartin o' opening your spiritual top-lights; haint I seen 'em do it? an haint I a right to convart you too, you red-livered land grampus? Look, your brother swabs yonder, are spying on you, an' envying your glory, so pump away, an' take in a fresh cargo like a christian, and don't be sufferin' such all-fired stuff to be wastin' down the bank yonder."

Crockett and Ben Hardin, "Going Ahead" of a Steamer

You see as how I war cradled by the Mississippi, schooled among her holler log canoes, an' tharfore, I'm a hull double bilered steamboat at a row or paddle; an' my old salt water friend, Ben Hardin, is nearly half equal to me. Ben and me went to take passage down the Big Muddy on a late occashun, in one o' them locomotive river towns called a western steamer; but we were refused a berth bekase we had a barr in our company, an' I wanted a berth for him along with myself. Taking this anti-republican refusal as an insult to my Congressional dignity, as well as to my well-bred pet Death Hug, Ben an' me detarmined to revenge our insulted respectability on 'em by beatin thar double-breasted steamer down the river by an independent private conveyance, built on our own hook entirely.

So we walked out to the woods, cut down a very ancient holler gum tree, cut it open one side, corked up both ends, cut a pair o' ten feet paddles, an' launched her into the Mississippy,

jist as the great steamer got out o' sight. I took old Death Hug aboard, put him at the starn, an' made him sit thar, an' hold up the pole o' Uncle Sam's flag, an' steer with his tail. Ben and I lit our great bowl pipes, took our paddles near the bow, an' the way we made 'em walk in an out the water made the fish stare, an' the banks o' Old Muddy fly behind us as fast as if etarnity war comin' all at once; an' we made the smoke roll up from our pipes thick enough to choke a common steambiler. Death Hug held up our flag, grinned, and steered us with his sweepin' tail as straight as a chalk line, an' take my paws for steamer paddle wheels, if in two hours we didn't pass the tarnal aristycratical steamer in sassy triumph, while Ben puffed his smoke at 'em, and I waved my Crockett flag, an' grinned victory.

Well, you see, arter beatin thar steamer with our holler gum tree into teetotal disgrace, I took a notion to build a regular independent steamer o' my own, to avoid all insults to my pet Bruin an' myself, for I always have my bear with me for company. So I jist went an' caught a ninety feet alligator, split him apart, an' hollered him out, arter which I sowed his two halves together, then dried it for about six months in our old smoke house, seasoned it with snapping turtle taller, till it war as hard as the hinges on etarnity. I then put a five hundred horse power steam engine into it, flattened its back into a deck, shod it with oak plank, hoisted Uncle Sam's flag, took Death Hug for helmsman and have used it ever since as a steam packet up and down the Big Muddy. And if ever war breaks out between Uncle Sam and any other nation, I mean to cut port holes in her sides, ship about fifty cannon, and set up a man o' war on my own hook.

Ben Hardin Carrying On

Once when I was cruising down the Mississippy on a raft, I fell in with a roaring feller in them parts, and arterwards I found out he was Kurnel Krockett; a glorious prize he was and had more whiskey in his barrel than some craft has when they are going on a India viage. So I kept my land tacks aboard till I had sounded the old feller pretty well, and found him a wise one—you know it takes a long head to make a Allmynack. Well, I seed very little of the Kurnel arterward till I started on my last viage. When we was out to sea, I fell from aloft and broke both legs, and put my hip out of place. I thort this misfortin was a sign that somethin bad was goin to happen, and true enuff, when I got home I heerd how my old friend the Kurnel had run agin a snag, as he used to call it, and had lost the number of his mess amongst the Texicans. It made me feel pleggy bad, and I went rite off and got drunk in honor of the Kurnel's disease. So I went on a cruise down into Kentuck, and there I come across the Kurnel's papers, so as I was knocked up with one game leg and a short hip, and as the doctor pronounced me unseaworthy, I thort I would keep up the Allmynack out of respect to the old Kurnel.

DAVY CONQUERING MAN

Crockett in a Fight with a Yankee

He grit his teeth at me, and poked out his tongue about six inches. With that I told him I was a pick-axe and would dig him out of his stumps. He said he was a flint image cut out of a big rock. I telled him my gizzard was a wasp's nest and I

breathed rifle balls. He said he could double up a streak o' lightning and thrash me with one eend of it.

Then I was pesky oneasy and spit at him so hard that if he hadn't dodged it, he'd have had his nose knocked flat. He came to me feet foremost, and I caught the great toe in my mouth, but the nail came off very lucky for him, and he got his toe

79

back again. But while he was bringing his foot to the ground, I caught the slack of his breeches in my teeth and lifted him up in the air, swinging like a scale beam, as if he didn't know which eend it was best to light on. But his trousers tore through in a minnit, and he come down sprawling.

He jumped up speechless, and looked around as amazed as if he war just born into the world. He seed I war jist ready to lay my paw on him agin, and his skin crawled. He turned as pale as a scalded nigger, and told the people that was looking on how they had better interfere as he wus afraid he should be the death of me, if we come to the scratch agin. I telled the lying sarpint to own he war chawed up, or I would make fiddle-strings of his tripe. So he squat low and felt mean. He sneaked off like an Injun in a clearing.

Crockett 'Pinking' an Indian

One morning early, as Crockett, with his dog Plump, started out in search of game, he accidentally fell in with a detachment of militia, who had encamped on the borders of a small yet deep river, so over-hung with stupendous rocky cliffs that an attempt to cross it would have been attended with certain death. The opposite bank was thickly covered with stumps and trees and a hostile Indian warrior was discovered among the stumps, reconnoitering their position; as soon as he was conscious that he had been seen, he tried to escape by practicing the wiles common to Indian warfare. He would throw himself flat on the ground behind a stump, so that no part of his body could be seen, where he would lie for a few minutes; then he would glide almost as fast as the lightning's flash, behind another. In this style he was in a fair way of reaching a covert of some bushes near at hand, notwithstanding several shots had been discharged at him by the soldiers—when Davy Crockett, who had been gazing on the scene, smiling at the ill success of the marksmen, said "I see I shall have to 'pink' that fellow; now look, and I will show you how it is done."

He caught up his rifle and directed it, not towards the

stump behind which the Indian was secreted, but towards the one where he supposed the Indian would next seek a shelter. In a moment afterward the Indian dashed from his hiding place —the sharp crack of Crockett's rifle was heard—and the Indian sprung several feet from the ground — uttered a loud yell — fell and expired, shot through the heart.

"There!" said David Crockett, with a hearty laugh, that shook the rock he stood upon, "that's what I call 'pinking' an Indian."

A Street Fight

Come next 17th of November, it will be jist ten years and forty-four days sence a squatter named Joe Jenkings transported his bacon into our settlement, and sot up within three miles of my cabin. I didn't like this notion of his'n at all, for my near nabors are all true grit and whole hearts except him. He had a down look as if he war setting traps, and he war much better at eating than he war at taking game. He had a voraciferous eye when it war open; but he never lookt a man in the face except it war pitch dark.

He had been in our parts about six months when he give out that he war going to have a great hunt with tame allygators. He said he had 'em in a pond near his cabin and that they would be all ready whenever the nabors would call, and that every one must bring a saddle and bridle. So when the day come, I and Zipperworth Blood, John Grace, Hornman Grizzle and about a dozen Suckers, Pukes and strangers went over to his place. His door was fastened, and thar war no smoke to be seen coming out of the top of the chimbly. So we pounded at the door, and I poked the end of Killdevil through the side of the cabin to stir him up; but he didn't come out, and we thort he might be gone down to feed his animals, and get the long-jawed varmints ready for the hunt.

Well, we put our butt eends upon a log, and waited for him to make his appearance. At last the sun got up over the top of the trees, and then we began to smell a rat. Zipperworth Blood put his foot agin the door as if he war kicking a mammoth, and it jumped off the hinges like a reformed office-holder. Then we bundled into the cabin, and found the pesky squatter had gone off with all his plunder, and had chalked out half a duzzin great allygators on the wall. We seed we had been fooled, and then we biled rite off. It war bad enuff to be fooled by a genuwine son of Kaintuck, but to be sarved such a trick by this lousy, ignorant, unsuspicious heathen varmint, war more than I could stand.

I jumped rite up and hit my head agin the roof. "Come," sez I, "and lets sally out and go arter him, and if I git sight of a piece of him, as big as a miskeeter's liver, I'll plaster it over with cold lead."

We screamed nine times and set out on the run. Some run up to Gum Swamp to see if the feller warn't hid among the bushes, and some others sallied up to the head of Salt River; but the pesky nigger was gone, and we went back and pulled his house down, to show proper resentment.

I went home in a very oneasy temper, and swore terrificasciously in my sleep, and vowed that I would shoot the fust squatter as showed his nose in the clearing agin. My wife put a hot brown bread poultice on my stomach to keep my gall from busting and withed my hands behind my back so that I needn't gouge her eye out when I war dreamin' about the heathen varmint. I give up the thort of ever seeing him agin, but I chalked up his name over my door, and vowed that I'd lick him in t'other world, if I never found him in this.

*

About seven years arter all this happent I cut out for Washington, to represent Old Kaintuck in Congress. I war obleeged to pare my thumb nail and put on a white shirt when I went there. It come very hard to me, but I knowed it war all for the good of my country, and so I did it. When I war in Washington, I war invited to all around, and seed a great menny fine folks, but they didn't know much, and thar war ladies thar that didn't know how to dress a possum, nor to gut a bear if it war already kilt to their hand.

Well, I war walking down Pennsilvany avennoo one day with two other members of Congress, and I seed a pesky shabby looking feller rite ahead of us, and I didn't like his looks. In a minnit or two he turned around, and who should it be but Joe Jenkings, the pesky squatter what sarved us sich a trick. I knowed him as soon as I seed his sheep's eyes, the white-livered varmint. I jist broke away from the other members, and run up to the feller and clapped my hands agin my side, and crowed in his face with all my mite.

With that, my two friends come up and one of 'em laid his hand on my sholder and sez, "What's the matter, Crockett. Remember where you be. You are in the most public street in Washington!"

"Stand back, gentlemen," sez I, "and form a ring, for here is goin' to be a training directly."

And then I jumped off the ground my whole length, and lit on the squatter like a drop of rain. He seized the waistbands of my breeches as I come down, and I stuck my thumb in his eye; he roared out like a bull, and tried to punch me in the bowels with one fist. By this time the people had gathered around us like it war a gin'ral 'lection, and every one said it war the fust time they seed a member of Congress who had any spunk. Pretty soon I got the squatter down, and jist then he fixt his teeth into my throte, and I felt my windpipe begin to loosen. I kept my thumb in his eye, and war jist going to give it a twist and bring the peeper out, like taking up a gooseberry in a spoon, when a member of Congress cotch'd hold of my coat tail; but he tore off the skirt and discombobolated my hold on the feller's eye, without hauling me off. Then the varmint seized my by the pantaloons and tore 'em clean off. In this way we kept lying on the ground till we war both covered with dirt and blood. Everybody come to see us fight, bekase I war a member of Congress, and when they pulled me off the squatter, all my close war tore off but my shirt.

The squatter war took up for dead. His nose war knocked

to one side, and looked as crooked as a pesky Gum Swamp
Injun's heart, and one of his eyes stuck out like a lobster. Some
of the folks talked of putting me up for President bekase I
had showed myself a military hero; and if this rencounter
don't make me one, thar's no snakes in Varginy, or weazels in
the Allegany Mountains.

Stopping a Duel Among His Brother Congressmen

I go most teetotalaciously agin that genteel kind of human
murder called duelling. I can shoot a bear or a painter most
splendiferous, but when it comes to standin' up coolly an' shootin' a human, an' about an article called honor, what nobody
cares about him that will murder, why it's a tarnal sight worse
than injuns.

One day at Washington arter an arternoon's loud talkin',
several of us Congressmen war in a room together talkin' of
public rogues, polytics, cards, an' tobacco. Two members got
quarrelin' about thar character, a thing which neither on 'em
had to my sartin knowledge, so I set over in the left corner
of the room, and eyed 'em slantendicularly; big words and
big faces follered each other, till directly one chap locked the
door and lifted his mouth pan to do the handsome thing, in
the shape of a back hander, when his more civilized opponent
cotched his arm an pulled out one o' them contemptacious,
cowardly little murderers machines, called pistols, and chal-
lenged him to murder, or in pure common talk to fight a duel.
Thar old Salt River gin to rise up in me, and instantly I walked
in between 'em.

"Gentlemen," says I, "I'm Davy Crockett, the darling branch
o' old Kentuck, that can eat up a painter, hold a buffalo out
to drink, and put a rifle ball through the moon. You may fight
fistifferously, kick hossiferously, or bite catifferously, but if you
attempt to murder another accordin' to fashion or broadcloth

84

honor, you'll find that Col. Crockett's a gentleman accordin'
to natur, an' won't tolerate any unnatural civilities between
nobody, coon killer or Congressman. I'll take you both across
my knee, scald all the clothes off of you, and kick you all the
way home; if I don't then cut me up for injun rations."

And I gin 'em one o' my alligator grins that made 'em all
hold on to thar hair for fear it would all fly out. Seeing I war
all blood, tooth an' detarmination, they chucked their pistols
into the fire, took a four inch chaw of tobacco, axed each
other's pardon, begged mine, and all give three shakin' cheers
for Colonel Crockett an' no duellin'. If they didn't, then grind
me up for cannon fodder.

Settling A Puke

One day as I war settin' in the door of my cabin, and sharpening out my thum nail, I felt wolfish about the head and
shoulders, when I seed a Puke and a Wolverine goin' by. The
Puke cocked his eye, and looked sassy. I looked at him and
snorted like a wild hoss.

Sez he—"I guess you feel wholesome this mornin'."

Sez I—"I feel as if I could double up any Puke that ever
walked between here and a generation of vipers."

That made him feel ugly, and he moved his ears like a jack-
ass, and sez: "Stranger, I think I shall go home with one of
your eyes in my pocket."

I stood up and spit in his face. He pulled up his breeches,
and crowed three times. I felt my flesh crawl over, and my toe-
nails moved out of place. I moved my elbow in scientific order,
and got ready to take a twist in his hair. When he seed that,
he squealed and ran around me three times. I jumped up, and
planted my heels in his bowels. That made him feel dissatis-
fied with me, and he caught me 'round the thigh and war
goin' to throw me down; but I stooped over and cotched him
by the seat of his trowsers and held him up in the air, when
he squirmed like an eel, and tried to shoot me with his pistol.

I twisted him over, and took his knee-pan in my mouth and bit clear through to the bone. He squawked and begged for mercy, and then I let him down, and give him a kick that sent him half a rod, and he run like a deer.

A Black Affair

I had just got afloat on the Great Bend, in my Alleghany skiff, and was about pushing off, when I seed the reeds bending most double, a trifle from the landing place. So I brought my rifle to bear and was just about getting a blizzard at the cretur, when it popped up its head, and I seed by the wool on the skull that it was a pesky great bull nigger.

"Blackey," says I — for I wanted to talk civil to it — "what may be your business jest now along shore and down among the reeds, with your two eyes sticking out like a panther's?"

With that he begun to look real saucy and grinned like a log house on fire. So says I to him, "It's no use Mr. Nig, or whatever your name is, to come the possum over me. I'm jest from Roaring River, wide awake and duly sober, and don't feel afeared of any nigger that ever slept between here and the other side of the eend of the yearth. So cut dirt, or by gum, I'll bark you clean from the end of your nose to the tip of your tail."

With that he looked as dumb as a wooden clock, and I thought the feller was going to hang fire. But instead of that, he edged along, and give a spring into my skiff, and ketched the long pole, and give the skiff a reverend set right out toward the middle of the stream. This was too much to take from a nigger no how, so I raised my rifle and was jest going to drop him into the water, when I hearn a low growl behind me, and when I turned round, though I kept one leetle corner of my eye on the nigger all the time, I seed a great black bear coming up to take the nigger's part. So, seeing they were birds of a feather, I thought best to let the nigger go a piece and try to kill the four-legged varmint, because if I didn't kill him

86

he might kill me, and I thought that would be most ridiculous. I let strip, and the ball hit the bear on the eend of the nose. So he stood right up on his hind legs, like a Congressman when he ketches the speaker's eye, and I seed there was going to be a serious misunderstanding between us right off, for my rifle was fired off, and the nigger had gone with the skiff; so I was a sort of forced to stand up to my lick log, salt or no salt. Then when I seed his great nails that sprawled out like a lobster's claws sharpened to a point, I thought he might have all my old moccasins and welcome, if he would only put them on. I took my rifle by the barrel and intarmined to explunctify his seven senses by a rap on the head.

Well, he jumped right at me with his mouth wide open. I happened to slip and didn't get a chance to take good aim. I hit him on the ribs and he squalled right out like an old woman at an awakening. But I pitched head foremost into the muss, and when that etarnal nigger seed me fall, he thought I was a gone sucker, so he come right back with the skiff to steal my rifle and powder horn, as soon as the bear should finish his breakfast off my ribs. The bear grew sort o' careless too when he saw that I was down, and this gave me a chance to haul out my knife which I whipped into his belly and deprived him of his bowels. The varmint couldn't do much arter he was fairly cleaned out inside, and he laid pretty still.

So I cocked my eye at Snowball then, and when he tried to give a set with the pole, he was in such a flustification that he fell into the water, and the skiff shot out into the stream about ten foot. So I was all ready for the pesky black thief, and stood close to the shore to tree him in good arnest when he landed. He seed me waiting for him and grinned like a steel trap. Up he came out of the water like a mad alligator, and I stood by as fierce as the latter eend of an airthquake.

In the first place I ketched him by the wool and jerked out two hands full, which made him feel quite unpleasant. He then run off and come at me with his head. He got hold of my two ears and gave me a butt right in the front part of my head, that enermost blinded me, for the feller's skull was as hard as the two sides of an iron pot. So I got one of my ears out of his infarnal black paw, and then I got two good blows at him with my feet on his shins. That made him so mad that he run his fingers right up my nostrils. I didn't mind that much, for it shut out the enduring bad smell which the cretur had about him when he got fairly warm.

So we wrassled and jerked and bit for a long time, till I got a chance at one of his eyes with my thum nail. Then when I begun to put on the rail Kentucky twist, he knew it was all day with him, and he fell on his knees and begged for mercy. I telled him to confess everything or I would snap his eye right out. So he owned that he had been out all night on a stealing excursion, and was trying to find has way to the swamp; he agreed to let me tie him up with grape vines, and I made the varmint fast, and put him into the skiff and carried him home. I seed the nigger once more when I was on my way to Congress, and he squinted most ridiculous.

This was the fust fight I ever had with a nigger, and I hope it will be the last, for the way I like to have got starved out with his cussed strong smell was a caution to a skunk. But if he hadn't confessed, I would have made him so near-sighted that he couldn't have seen a whip till he felt it.

A Big Lie

The biggest lie that war ever told in Kaintuck, war that of an infarnal Puke at the 'lection, who war telling some of his comrades that Kurnell Crockett refused his whiskey to a stranger; but I stood right behind him, and jist tapped him on the head. He lookt round and cotch sight of my thumb nale, when he said, "I meant a Kurnell Crockett that used to peddle small wares, from Connecticut."

Col. Crockett and the Squatter

Once upon a time Kongress made a law to give away part of the public lands in old Kentuck — that is, if a feller could prove that he'd made an improvement and growed corn on it, he was to have the first rite to buy. They called this the rite of preemption, which war no rite at all in some cases; as I shall exemplify to you presently.

One day in 1829 Jim Hickory came into my clearing, the same Jim they called the Riproarer of Salt River, and axed me if I knowed the Piankashaw Bottom on Bears Grass, and the places adjacent.

"Do you think Davy Crockett's a fool?" sez I.

"No," sez he, "I wouldn't be so imperlite as to say that, and it would be a d--d lie if I did; but the fact ar, I'm going to buy the bottom off the land agent, and I want your testification that I had an improvement thar."

"When war that, Jim?" sez I. "I never heerd tell of it before."

"It war between 1825 and 1826," sez Jim.

"Now, Jim, I won't be such a blackguard as to tell you you lie," sez I, "or anything of that ar sort; but it ar a fact, you don't speak the truth, or anything within a thousand mile of it. You know you war gone to Santa Fee that ar year."

"Kurnul," sez he, "that's a small bit of a mistake."

"Do you mean to tell me I lie?" sez I; "because if you do there will be trouble between us in less time than hell would scorch a feather!" (Lord forgive me for swearing — it ar a thing I'm not used to; but it made my bristles stand rite up to think Jim wanted me to swear to a no-such-a-thing.)

"Kurnel," sez Jim, for he see that my temper war in a state of pretty considerable mollification; "I don't want to entice you to do anything agin your conscience. Just go with me to the ground, and if I don't satisfy you I had corn growing thar between twenty-five and six, I'll give you my skin to make razor strops of, that's all."

Well, thought I, it will do no harm to go with him, any how he can fix it; and as it war a magnificent day, I shouldered old

Killdevil and went along with him. When we got to the spot, he had built up a shanty there, and had a cow, and showed me three stalks of corn growing between two pepperage trees. "Thar," sez he, "Kurnel, did you ever see finer corn in your life?"

"The corn ar well enuff," sez I; "but it war not growing here three or four year ago, for sartin."

With that the infarnal varmint showed me whar he had cut 1825 and 1826 in great figures on the trees with his knife, and the corn war growing between them, sure enuff, and then I begun to feel awful conscientious.

"Look you, Jim Hickory," sez I: "you've barked up the wrong tree this time. Do you know what you've done, you cussed, illiterate, unscrupulocious offscowring of creation and crooked barrel of a shotgun? You've axed Davy Crockett to swear to a lie. Don't come for to go to be wolfy or cantankerous at what I say; for there can't be no scalping between us. I stand on the character of a gentleman and the universal dignity of human natur, and I can't condescend to chaw you up, for you're no gentleman, and what's more, no man — not the least indefinite article of a man. You're a fool and can't dance, and your daddy's got no peach orchard, and I think it ar my duty to bring you to justice. Do you see what that cow has just let drop? It ar not honey or apple sarse, ar it? Now if you don't sit down and eat every atom of it, I'll make daylite shine through you quicker than it would take lightning to run round a potato patch."

And so I cocked my rifle and drew a lead on the white of his eye. Jim didn't much like to do it, but he seed my back was up, and he knew there was no mistake about Davy Crockett. He tried hard to beg off, but that was neither here nor there, and so, as there was no help for it, rather than have his soul-case bored through with my screw auger, he sot down to his confectionary, and I didn't spare him a spoonful of it, though he did make awful ugly faces. He was so ashamed of the whole affair that he axed my pardon for what he'd done, and I never had a better friend arterwards. I kinder think he'll never forget the taste of perjury as long as he lives.

Struggle with the Indian Chief "Wild Cat"

You've no doubt heered of "Wild Cat," the chief of the sassiest tribe o' sausage colored niggers that ever split a skull, or breakfasted on the warm blood of white-faced human nater. Well, he was a tee-total death to every crittur in the Kentuck forest, excepting wildcats, and them he always respected an' protected, because he had an idea that they were closely akin to him on his father's side. The critter knowin' that I went in for using up his four-legged long-clawed cousins, he determined to find me out, an' drink me up hull in my own gravy.

Well, being out one mornin' hunting for sport, I scalped an old he wildcat, one of his second cousins, clar down to the neck, and made a nice cap which I put on my head, as a sign of victory and defiance o' the hull wildpuss nation, Indian relatives and all. I war jist scaling up a tree to look out for new sport, when thar sat the tarnal Chief "Wild Puss," with his eyes stickin' out as long as his knife. Seeing the head and scalp of one of his relatives stuck fresh and bloody on the top of my oak knot, he pointed at it, and howled all sorts of red malice at me, while I patted the puss's topknot and grinned all sorts of tantilization at him. At me he come; and into him I went; and the way we hugged and gouged, made the old tree smoke and shake agin; an' he war jist sendin' his corn-knife into the Mississippy o' my juglar vein, when I grabbed him by the neck like any other pussy an' squeezed it into dislocation, kicked his backbone out o' jint, and sent him down, howlin' mercy, till he bussed a rock about ninety feet below, split his brains, and knocked out his nine lives beautiful.

(Illustration on following page)

91

Colonel Crockett's Trip to Texas and Fight with the Mexicans

I'm a hull team of a patriot myself, from the eend of my biggest hair to the pint of my big toe nail; and when any tyrant takes a liberty with the nateral liberty of man, it rises the Mississippi o' my Yankee blood into a perfect freshet, and I'm ready to sweep away all tyrannical corruption as clean as Noah's flood. Considering Texas as one o' the stars that belonged to Uncle Sam's Striped Handkerchief, I swore, by the hem in Freedom's buckskin petticoat, that Santa Ann or any other tyrant should never wipe his nose with it; and hearin' that the etarnal Mexican Satan was about making another scheme to steal it and the little farm to boot, I recollected the all-bloody lickin' I gin him at Alamo, buckled on my old scythe which he knows is about equal to old death, and prepared to start off instanterly to carve the whiskered critter right up. So I jist sharpened my teeth on one o' my flyin' millstones, bolted up a little Yankee lightnin', an' bridled a he barr that I had larn't to outrun a thunderbolt, and put out like a high pressure hurrycane for Texas.

Now this barr o' mine had caught a bit o' my indignation, and the way he sweat, grunted, and made the rocks an' trees fly behind him, made the very hair o' creation stand straight up in double distilled wonder. An' by the time that we landed in Texas, his etarnal speed had scalded all the hair from his back an' set my buckskins all in a smoke. The very ground and trees knowed me the very moment I arrived, an' all seemed to shout, "Etarnal Freedom, for Davy Crockett's come."

Well, smellin' which direction old Santy and his whiskered shootin' flock laid, I put out arter 'em, findin' 'em instanterlike — an' by the Big Alleghany, if ever a set of feathered mortals cut stick they did. But it war no more use than a big goose hissing at thunder, for I out with my bone scythe, an' if I didn't make Mexican heads fly about as thick as horsechestnuts in a hurrycane, then melt me into iron for steambilers. I fed five hundred flocks o' wolves on their meat, made a thousand quail traps o' their bones, wiped the sweat off with Uncle Sam's Striped Handkerchief, and come home to Kentuck as fresh as old Niagara.

Crockett Playing Death with the Mexican Pirates

I always thought as how the tarnal Injuns war the all-blood drinkin' savagest rascals o' the human creation, but the pirates are the human painters o' the seas, as I'll jist tell. You see on my trip to Texas I got sea-sick, that it turned my etarnal in- tarnals inside out, and I had to get a hull crew o' sailors to turn me back again. So arter I landed at Texas, I thought I had better take a little bit of a reglar sea excursion, for to salt my blood agin; so I jist got into a boat by myself, and sculled her about the old sea like a cork on the water, for every time the old sea got his froth up and growed sassy, I jist slapped him in the face, and made him lay down as quiet as a mill dam.

Well, one night, I heered a ship near me, an' a tarnal great screechin' o' voices, so I jist give a kick at the sea behind me, and sent my canoe in that direction. The nigher I got the thicker the screams come, and dreckly I heard a pop from one of their loud cast-iron shootin' sticks, and by the big flash I seed a hull nest o' these Mexican yaller jackets, or sea painters, creeping from one ship into another; an' the shootin' an' screamin' o' women beat a hull creation o' wildcats treed by a thousand Kentuck hunters. My Mississippi o' humanity couldn't stand that 'ere; I pulled to the ship, mounted her as a cat would a crab apple tree, swung out my oak tree war club, an' the way I made them Mixican cats knock out thar nine lives against the floor of the vessel, was equal to a broad- side o' Captain Stockton's* big guns. I stove one feller's head clean into his shoulders out o' sight, an' the piratical juice run out like cider from a screw press. I killed two chaps that had

*Robert Field Stockton, naval officer prominent in the Mexican War.

94

DAVY CROCKETT CUDJELING THE PIRATES IN THE GULF STREAM.

gals by the hair, an' presarved thar sweet lives, hair and all.

I then went down stairs, and thar I found two lions that jist broke loose, and war coming up to take a supper on fresh pirate meat. I lugged both by the hair into their iron cabin, put the ship to rights, and steered right straight for Texas; and when I landed, I harnessed them and presented them to General Houston for his private baggage waggon. If I didn't, then feed me on pirate scythes.

Crockett Out-Diving the Pearl Divers

When I was a youngster, Ben Hardin' an' myself happened to be landed from a ship on the coast of Japan, where there were a whole flock of the yeller-skinned natives, without clothes enough on their backs to cover a sucking pig. They were called "Divers," an' made thar living by diving down into the oyster-beds, for oyster-pearls, an' the feller that can dive the deepest, an' stay dived the longest, gets the most pearls, an' is quite a pearl among the people.

Thar was a pearl merchant on the spot, making mighty tall bids for the precious article, an' thar was a diver that was famous for staying two minutes under the natural pickle-tub, but he didn't seem to have any sort of luck in his oystering expedition. So, taking a sharp look at the natur of the beach, I told Ben to hold my hat an' life insurance, while I made a trip below, an' in I went. I soon fotch'd bottom at the mouth of a sort of a cave like the "hole in the ground" in old Kentuck. I crawled along it until I got into dry land under water; made a lamp-wick out of a lock of my hair; soaked it in some elbow-grease; struck a light with my flint on a rock, an' I discovered that I had got among thousands of pearl oysters, fast asleep in their beds,—but they were all "wide enough awake" to close thar mouths about as tight as a money market in a pressure. So I went to work, an' danced the Kentucky reel on top of 'em, so all-kicking strong, that they all opened their jaws with the force of the heat like a clamb-bake; an' the way

I went to work an' pulled out the pearls was like geese pecking up corn. Having got as large a majority as I could float with, I steered up for Terra Firma, after being under pickle just eleven hours an' three quarters. When I landed, I found the natives firing guns to bring up my dead body; an' Ben Hardin was writing a dead letter home to Mammy Crockett. I sold pears enough to buy a whole ship, paid a diver's fee to the natives, who fell down and gave three rounds of grunts for Davy Crockett, the pearl of all pearl divers.

Crockett and the Black Emperor of Hayti

When I was in Hayti some years ago, I happened to come in contact with its black emperor Soulouque, the Prince of Niggers, as well as a Nigger of a Prince. Although pretty rank, he is very sweet for a darkey, an' cultivates the sugarcane about as tall as we Southern Yankees grow cotton. He is allfired sweet on his many sugar-fields, but being a black, he is opposed to making white sugar; an' so he converts all the juice of the cane into brown sugar, rum, an' molasses.

Well, you see, I was one day riding along the road, by a pretty tall cane-field, an' my horse, being of the old Tennessee breed, had a sweet tooth in his head, an' scenting the sugar plant as if he was at home, turned right into a plantation-gate an' commenced chawing away at the sugar-cane about as sassy an' swaggerous as a sugar press. I sat still, perfectly docile, an' let him have his rein, an' the way he went into devouriation made all the black sarpent planters' eyes stick out like double-breasted geese eggs. The black critturs made some pesky ugly faces, an' grinned all sorts of opposition. I only smiled pretty tall, an' the horse merely snorted a few, and went on with his sweet provender to the tune of "King Chaw-chaw."

After a small while, I saw the niggers all pointing in a sartain direction, an' in a few minutes along came a great, gaunt, gawkey-looking nigger, on a nigger horse. The feller had more

97

feathers in his hat than twenty Injuns; more stars an' gilding on his coat an' breeches than twenty play-actors; an' his boots were kivered over with breast-pins. I soon heerd that the said individual, boots an' all, was the emperor Soulouque; an' down fell all the darkies on their hands an' knees, or their stomachs. Seeing that I didn't follow suit in the ceremony, he rode up to me, an' spluttered out, "I am the mighty Emperor of Hayti; down on your knees!"

I merely said, "I am Col. Davy Crockett, one of the sovereign people of Uncle Sam, that never kneels to any individual this side of sunshine."

With that he gave an order to his hull field-population, an' at me they came; they all came with clubs, cords, an' cane-cutters. Well, I just took an' pulled up a couple of hard sun-dried canes by the roots, dashed in among 'em, an' the way I sugar-caned that entire nigger creation, Emperor an' all, out of them diggings, was equal to Sampstrong among the Philistines.

Crockett Among the Cannibals

When I war quite a saplin', Ben Hardin and I took a trip to the Sandwich Islands, and a few days afore our reckoning, we made land by striking a rock that split our ship like a close-grained fence-rail all into bits, too pesky small for any human crittur to hold on to. After swimmin', divin', sharkin', fightin',

99

and killin' about in the open sea for three days, we were surrounded by about fifty he and she cannibals, and dragged to the den of these all-greedy gobbling, human-natur eating niggers.

Now I reckon my flesh at that time must a been a sort of delicate an' temptin', for I seed by peepin' through a small corner of my left eye, that their confounded cannibalesses war making up a plot to eat me right off for a tit bit. I let 'em go on till I got purty well rested an' my indignation up to bilin' pint, and jest as they were walkin' into me, boots, breeches, and all, I sprung up, grabbed 'em by the hair, and slung 'em about till I shook the wind and teeth out o' 'em. I then went to Ben Hardin, waked him up; we grabbed a few old spears in the cabin, and the way we treated the sharks to a cannibal supper has been a terrification to the hull creation o' cannibals.

Crockett's Recipe for Cooking Bear-Steak

Salt 'em in a hail storm, pepper 'em with buckshot, an' then broil 'em with a flash o' lightnin'!

Crockett Killing Four Wolves at the Age of Six

Once I war riding through the forest, when I war about six year old, as I expected to see Zip Wing, who war about my age in them days, tho' he is older now, and I heered something holler. I thought it war Zip, and I punched my horse with my knife to make him go faster. In a little while I seed the bushes stir, and the next minnit a pesky great wolf come out and jumpt right at the horse. The horse kicked him over, but he got up again and howled most beautiful. Three other wolves heered him when he howled, and they all come running as if a hornet had lodged under their tails.

As soon as they seed me and the horse, they sot up a howl and jumpt at us with their mouths wide open. One of 'em cotch the sturrup in his mouth and tried to bite my leg off. I stuck the knife into the back of his neck, and he rolled over amongst the leaves. Another one jumpt rite up on the saddle behind me. That war the most impudentest thing that I ever knowed a varmint to do, and it made me so odoriferous mad that I jumpt rite forward on the horse's neck, and put a knife into his bowels; that give him the colic and set him to sneezing. The horse cotch one of the wolves in his teeth and bit out his windpipe, and tother one I shot with my rifle.

A Squabble with Two Bears

One day I told my dog Tupe to follow me, put my rifle on my shoulder, and filled my jug with whisky, and sallied out to kill something for my bowels, for I had felt rather dainty for some time, having lived mostly on biled acorns and rattlesnake chowder. I struck out a new path. The reader knows war Frog Bend crosses Gum Swamp, up near the head of great Mud Turtle Fork. Well, I went up that way, in hopes of seeing some wild ducks, which are very partial to them parts, bekase the crack of Davy Crockett's shooting iron is heered thar but seldom.

When I got up near the river side, I lookt all around and all asquare, and couldn't see nothing to draw a lead upon, without it war snakes, and they war so thick I trod on 'em at every step I took; but Tupe seemed to be inkurriged, and every once in a while he made a noise like thar war work to be done. So I kept on, for thar ar no back out in my breed, more than a cannon ball will turn a corner and retreat in the face of the enemy. At last I picked out the softest stone I could find, and sot down upon it. I laid down my rifle, turned up Brown Betty, and sucked in about half a pint of the most precious licker that ever run through the neck of a bottle.

Well, I sot thar lookin' out upon the river, and thinking about nothin', when I seed the shadder of a cretur's head rite down before me. I turned round my head and thar war two big black bears looking over the top of my raccoon cap, as gravitatious as the speaker of the House when he gives his casting vote. The biggest one of these varmints had my rifle in his mouth, a tryin to larn t'other one to take aim. Now that war too bad, and war showin contempt to me, and my rifle too; but the bear seed me as soon as I turned my eyes up and he lookt wonderous wise, you may be sure. I jumpt up and laid a heavy club over the cretur's head—he took the hint, dropt my rifle, and made a dive for the river. I threw down my rifle, and touched Big Butcher to see if all war rite, and then I dove into the river like a mad alligator.

The bear swum faster than I could, and he went rite up the stream, but a floating log war coming down the tide, and he war obleeged to sheer out; so I got jist up to the eend of his tail, and set my teeth into it like the lockjaw. He swum a little ways, and turned round to make me let go. He showed his two rows of ivory, and snarled most butiful. Then I let go his tail, and sunk rite under his belly, and drawed Big Butcher. When I whipt it into his bowels he grunted and whirled about, and made a dive at me. We war soon tryin to git on top of one another, and my cloze war tore into strips. The water wur red by this time, and thar war a great deal of hugging, and pesky little love about it. Sumtimes the bear got my head under water, and when I tried to put my knife into his guts, he would have his paw upon mine, and a very leetle scratch of a bear's paw will let out a man's intestines.

But jist as I got a chance to shove the knife up to the hilt in his heart, and while it war going through his pesky soul-case, I heered a rifle go off, and at the same time, a piece of cold lead went into the fleshy part of my shoulder. I took the dead varmint by one ear and snaked him ashore with me, and as soon as I landed, thar war a pesky Squatter with his gun, who begin to lay claim to the bear. He swore he shot the animal with his rifle.

"Stranger," sez I, "if you don't make tracks faster than ever you did in your life, I'll send you into eternity along with this varmint, in jist half no time at all."

That lifted his dander rite up, and he swore he war seven devils, with a dozen steamboats in tow, all under high pressure, and vowed that I didn't kill the bear, and said he saved my life, for the bear would a' killed me, if he hadn't shot him. Then I jist shoved my four-finger into my shoulder and took out his ball, and showed it to him, on the palm of my hand. The feller felt so small that he had to look rite up over his head to see me, and crawled off like a lizard.

Shaving a Painter

When I lived up near the great fork o' Red River, thar war a goose stolen from my pen every nite, so I watched all one nite, with Killdevil, to see if I could ketch the critter. At about one in the morning, I seed a big painter leap over into the pen and pick out the fattest goose he could find, and carry it off. On the next nite, I sot a trap, and there war the painter as large as life. I war so mad that my skin crawled, and my hair stood up like pine groves in winter, for the cretur looked me in the face as innocent as if he had never took a goose in all his life. I thought it war too merciful to shoot him; so I jist got a rope over his legs, an' tied him up, an' then I got my razor an' shaved all the hair off his body, from his nose to the end o' his pesky tail, an' he kept up such a terrificacious yelling all the time that they heard it clear up in Pine Hollow. When I let him loose with all the hair shaved off, his skin war as smooth as a gal's cheek, and the crittur didn't know what to do. He kept turning round and round, an' was so ashamed that he kivered up his face with his paws. My wife and darters come out an' laft at him, an' then he sot out an' run into the forest. I don't think he ever come back into them parts, for the crittur war ashamed to be seen.

Adventure with a Rattlesnake

It come on to rain one day while I war in the woods. Now Kurnel Crockett war never afeared of a wet skin; but I had some powder with me that I wanted to keep dry; and so I looked round for a place to squeeze into, and I soon got squint of a small opening in the rocks, whar I could jist squeeze my body in. So I pushed in my rifle, and then crept in on my hands and knees. I found the place run in a good ways under ground, and so I went and wriggled in as fur as I could git. I hadn't been thar long before I heered something rattle, and when I lookt up thar war a pair of specks of fire looking right at me. I knowed then, it war a rattlesnake, and them varmint are a screamer. They are as smooth and as dangerous as a Yankee pedlar; and if they bite, it is a smart chance of pison that goes into your vitals.

Now, I was jammed in between the rocks, and couldn't turn round, and couldn't git hold of my rifle. I couldn't crawl back-foremost before he would be on me. So I war obleeged to stand up to my lick log. At last I fixed upon my weapons, and begun to grin. I had heered of some fellers that could grin the bark off a tree, and I was no little one at it myself. So I begun the real ripsnorting, rantankerous grin. I grinned till my nose bled, and it loosened two of my teeth, and made my shirt collar stand up

as stiff as a centre board. But it war no use, for the varmint begun to come closer and closer, so I seed thar war no way to git
clear in decent fashun, and I darted my head forward, and cotch
him with my teeth round his neck. I pressed my jaws together
till they met. It took him by surprise, for he thort he war going
to have his pesky fangs into me; and the way the varmint
sprung and thrashed, and twisted, would have most made some

folks let go. But I knowed if he got clear I war a gone case, so
I hung on upon his back with my teeth. While he war twisting,
he struck me two or three times on the head with his tail, and
it kindermost stunned me; for the cretur had no notion of dying
rite off, and I thort I must stay thar.

Then a smart idee come into my head, and I begun to back
out of the place, while I dragged him arter me by the teeth; but
every jerk he give almost hauled the head off my shoulders,
and I had a stiff neck for a year arterward. But I grinned and

stuck, till I got him into the open air, and then I cotch him by
the middle, and as I let go with my teeth, I slung him as fur as
I could. When he lit on the ground, I cotch up my rifle, and put
a charge of shot into his yaller hide, that made him jump a rod
right tother way. I stuffed his skin, and my wife wore it to
church for a tippet, a good many years.

Crockett's Account of a Bull Fight at New Orleans

The folks at New Orleans are the all-queerest mixture o' all
creations' population than can be found in or about any part
o' this here round-shoulder globe. They are about half Yankee,
half Mounseer, half Spanish, half Portugeese, half Indian,
half Nigger, an' t'other parts are a compound o' shark an' alligator, an' their Sunday go-to-meeting worship sports are made
up on a mixture of the usages an' pastimes of all these different hetrogenous nations, with a few trimmings of their own.

But their great boast and holiday glory is a Bull Fight, in the
reg'lar barbarous an' human nasty fashion o' old Spain. Well, I
went down to this half moon city some time ago, to make sale
of a few hundred barrels of alligator oil, and show my darter
Ann Crockett about city fashion and etticat. While thar I war
invited by a brother congressman to attend a bull fight, an' up
I went, expectin' to see something strong, manly and savarrag-
erous. Well, we got into a great round place with great rows of
pews, one above the other, and a ring in the middle.

In thar war some men with cat smellers on thar upper lips,
lookin' for all the world like half-singed painters. Well, these
he-human critters rapped their crooked sticks, a great cowbell
rung a few times, an' out come a few yeller lookin' human critturs, on horseback, dressed in green jackets and cloaks, with
them 'ere identical cat-smellers on their upper lips, and great
long poles in their hands, with a spear or prong at the end on it.
Arter throwing a tantalizing red cloak over the bull's face, they

then made at him with a sword, while the bull stumbled, hooked, pitched, foamed at the mouth an' nose, an' roared an' bellered worse than my old mammoth cow with the hollow horn. Directly long come the bull an' his man together rough and tumble, hook and stab, stab and hook again, till one or both rolled over kickin', bleedin', an' roarin'. Now an' then the poor horse would get a horn in his side an' rear up, kickin' an' yellin' like a prairie horse, and all the time the men and women in the pews would clap their paws, and shout and scream in all sorts of delighted refined humanity.

The folks all pitied the men, but Rockett Ann an' I pitied the poor dumb beef, for a more cowardly thing I never seed since my big ram butted the little one arter he war down — only to think of a parcel o' human critters calling themselves men, taking swords an' spears to flog a few bullocks with fightin' irons, instead o' attackin' them in the clear naked state of nature, claws, teeth an' toe-nails. The sight on it made me so courageous, that I jist laid my cravat and cap in Rockett Ann's lap, jumped into the ring, and crowed like a rooster.

"Now," says I, "strangers," says I, "jist drive me in a fresh flock o' bulls, with horns about as sharp as a bayonet, an' if I don't show you a fair sample of bull floggin' in the nat'ral way, then take my tongue for wheel straps."

Directly, the ring was cleared of fresh beef and human corpses, and in come three savagerous mammoth bulls. The people shouted, the bulls bellered, and I jumped; then I rubbed the sweat of my hands in the tar, and walked into 'em like a Kentucky beauty into fresh butter. First came the biggest animal of the three, and pitched into me with his right horn, aimed at the middle o' my digestion. I hit him with my fist, bang in the middle of his skull, and my foot in his paunch; he give a death grunt, turned pale at the nose, an' rolled over beautifully.

The people shouted. "Go it Dad," yelled Rockett Ann. I whistled an' danced ready for the other two, that now dashed at me right and left in a most sassagerous manner, squirting thar froth into my very mouth. I jist footed an' fisted, and both fell backward upon thar hind territories; then I jumped right

110

around, caught hold of thar two tails and swung 'em around the ring, till their ribs cracked agin each other, and then laid 'em down ready for skinning.

Crockett and the Boa Constrictor

One arternoon when I sallied out to cut some bear's meat, to entertain a brother member of Congress, who war at my cabin on a visit, I war looking up into a tree, when something slid out under me, and wound itself around my body so affectionate that at first I thought it war Mrs. Crockett herself. But when I felt how smooth the crittur war, I knowed it war a Yankee pedlar, or a snake. In a minute it had come up agin my cheek, and I seed that it war a pesky great snake. He looked at me right in the eye, and I looked at him, and we tried to stare one another out of countenance. I grinned at the cretur till he got mad, and then he opened his mouth. Before he could take in my head, I run my fist down his throat, and stuck Big Butcher into his pesky hide behind me. That loosened the varmint, and he unwound himself as fast as a Fork River gal takes off her garter the night after she is married. Mrs. Crockett made him into soup the same day.

I war pesky sore and tightly squeezed together by the critter, and the only way I could git myself in prime order agin, war to take a small run of about seven miles every morning for a week afterwards, which put my bones all in fine circulation.

A Sensible Varmint

Almost every body that knows the forest, understands parfectly well that Davy Crockett never loses powder and ball, havin' ben brought up to believe it a sin to throw away amminition, and that is the benefit of a vartuous eddikation. I war out in the forest one arternoon, and had jist got to a place called the Great Gap, when I seed a rakkoon setting all alone upon a tree. I clapped the breech of Brown Betty to my shoulder, and war jist a going to put a piece of lead between his shoulders, when he lifted one paw, and sez he, "Is your name Crockett?"

Sez I, "You are rite for wonst, my name is Davy Crockett."

"Then," sez he, "you needn't take no further trouble, for I may as well come down without another word." And the cretur walked rite down from the tree, for he considered himself shot.

I stoops down and pats him on the head, and sez I, "I hope I may be shot myself before I hurt a hair of your head, for I never had sich a compliment in my life."

"Seeing as how you say that," sez he, "I'll jist walk off for the present, not doubting your word a bit, d'ye see, but lest you should kinder happen to change your mind."

Col. Crockett Grinning a Grizzly Out of Countenance

You may say what you please and be d----d, Mr. Stranger, about your annycondy, your great terrificacious sarpint of Seelon in South Ameriky, and your rale Bengal tiger from Afriky. Both on 'em heated to a white heat and welded into one would be no part of a-priming to a grizzly bear of the Rocky Mountains. He'd chaw up your roonosseros and your lion and your tiger as small as cut tobacco, for breakfast, and pick his teeth with the bones. The cretur is rale grit and don't mind fire no more than sugar plums, and none of your wild animules can say that for themselves. I've killed one or two on 'em myself, which ar not a thing many Pukes or Suckers can boast on, tho they are pretty good at scalping injuns. I was delightfully skeeered by the fust I ever saw—no, that ar a d--d lie, tho I say it myself. Davy Crockett was never skeered by anything but a female woman; but it ar a fact that I war tetotaciously consarned for my life.

You see, when I war young I went for to massacree the buffaloes on the head of Little Great Small Deep Shallow Big Muddy River, with my nigger b'y Doughboy, what I give three hundred dollars for. I'd been all day vagabondizing about the prairie without seeing an atom of a buffalo, when I seed one grazing in the rushes on the edge of a pond, and a crusty old batchelder he was. He war a thousand year old at least, for his hide war all kivered with scars, and he had as much beard as would do all the dandies I've seen in Broadway for whiskers and mustashes a hull year. His eyes looked like two holes burnt in a blanket, or two bullets fired into a stump, and I seed he was a cross cantankerous feller, what couldent have no comfort of his life bekase he war too quarrelsome.

If there's ennything Davy Crockett's remarkable for it's for his tender feelings, speshally toward dumb creturs, and I thort it would be a mercy to take away his life, seeing it war onny a torment to him and hadent no right to live, no how. So I creeps toward him like a garter snake through the grass, trailin' Killdevil arter me. I war a going to tickle him a little about the short ribs jest to make him feel amiable, when out jumps a great bear, as big as Kongress Hall, out of the rushes and lights upon the old bull like a grey-winged plover. He only hit him one blow, but that war a side winder. I wish I may be kicked to death by grasshoppers if he didn't tear out five of his ribs and laid his heart and liver all bare. I kinder sorter pitied the old feller when I seed him brought to such an untimely eend, and I didn't somehow think the bear done the thing that war right, for I always does my own scalping and no thanks to interlopers.

So sez I, "I'm a civil man, Mr. Bear, saving your presence, and I wont come for to go to give you no insolatious language; but I'll thank you when we meet agin, not to disremember the old saying, but let every man skin his own skunks."

And with that I insinewated a ball slap through his heart. By the ghost of the great mammoth of Big Bone Licks, you'd have thort, by the way he gnashed his teeth, I'd a spoken something onpleasant to him. His grinders made a noise jest as if all the devils in hell war sharpening cross-cut saws by steam-power, and he war down upon me like the whole Missouri on a sand bar. There's no more back out in Davy Crockett than thar ar go-ahead with the Bunker Hill Monument, and so I give him a socdologer over his coconut with the barrel of old Killdevil that sot him a-considering, till he thort better on it and sot off after Doughboy as if the devil had kicked him on eend.

It's true Doughboy slipped a ball inter his ampersand jest as I struck him, but that war not what turned him; I grinned him out of countenance, so he thort it war safer to make his breakfast on Doughboy than me, which war a thing oncreditable to his taste, seeing I war a white man and he only a nigger. Well, I hadn't time to load my iron before he gathered upon Doughboy like a Virginny blood mare, and the nigger give himself up for a gone sucker, and fainted away. The bear got up to him jest as I war putting down my ball, and I expected to see him swaller the b'y without greasing; but he no sooner smelt of him than he turned up his nose in disgust and run away howling as if his delicacy was hugaceously shocked.

By this time I felt most enticingly wolfy and savagerous, and I jest give him a hint that no man could neglect that it war best to turn in his tracks, and I waited for him rite on the edge of Little Great Small Deep Shallow Big Muddy. He pitched inter me like the piston of a steam engine, and we both rolled into the drink together. Onluckily for him I didn't lose holt of Killdevil, and when he raised his head and tried to get over his astonishment, I clapt the barrel right across his neck to shove his visnomy* under water. I'll be shot with a packsaddle without benefit of clergy if the ridiculous fool didn't help me himself; for he clapped both hands on the eends of the barrel and pulled away as if it war a pleasure to him. I had nuthing to do but hold on to the stock and float alongside of him till he war drowned.

Don't you come for to say that I'm telling the least of a lie, for every fool knows a grizzly bear will live an hour with a ball through his heart, if so be he's only mad enuff.

Crockett's Pet Hyena

You see thar a likeness as large as life of a hyena that I tamed and made as domestic as a suckin' kitten. The extraordinary crittur could outlaugh an airthquake, and he war so all-kittishly wild that a nor'east wind couldn't reach him. The lightnin put arter him once, but he snorted it clar out o' countenance; an' when I come for him, we ran for seven days and nights, when he turned around, and spit a whole sea o' froth at me. But I jist run my fore-finger through his nose, making a nateral ring and led him home as docile as a frosted fly.

*Physiognomy.

Encounter with an Anaconda

While me an' Ben Hardin' was coasting about the shores of Brazil, I took a boat an' went ashore for some fresh water; an' arter I had swallowed about a cask or two, an' filled a couple more to take to the ship, I felt pretty tired an' sleepy. So I threw my head down upon a stone in the gunnel, and had just about started a sort of a snooze, when I felt as if something was bathing my feet with soapsuds. I popped up my head, an' by old thunder, what should I discover but about seventy feet of a snake of the reg'lar Antyconda tribe, with a head as big as a water-cask, eyes as big as bungholes smoking with red fire, an' a mouth an' jaws about as big as a loco-motive engine; an' there he was, licking my feet an' legs with his etarnal slippery-slimy snake-gravy, preparatory to swal-lerin' me hull, an' "suckin' me in" suddenaciously beautiful.

Now this was the very fust time in the hull o' my creation that I had ever been licked, an' it made me feel about as cross as three-pronged lightnin'. Well, I own up that at first I was a little bit stumped as to what I should do, an' the way I should do it; for I knowed that if I walked into him, an' we came to a clinch, the ugly crittur would come his contortion, contwisting an' hugging game, an' crush me clean up into Crock-ett jelly.

Luckily there happened to be a small one-pounder gun or swivel under the gunnel; I pulled it out as still as a mice; spilt a little stray powder into it that I happened to have in my shirt-pocket; knocked off a few bits of stone from my rock-pillow; poked them down the muzzle, powdered and primed. Just then he give my foot a lick with his tongue; I give him a kick; he poked up his head, grinning the hull infernal regions at me, an' was just about to make a particklar spring, when I struck fire with my knuckles, let go, and sent his head sailing amongst the buzzards.

116

Crockett and His Pet Alligator on an Exploring Expedition

You see, arter my great expedition to Texas on my wonderful barr, my helping to flog the Mexicans and ramsacking all the rivers to thar very springs spread Crockett's fame for enterprise all through the hull of South America. An' right off the Brazillian government sent for me to explore some o' thar etarnal, long, never-found out rivers, that belonged to the Tigers and Auntycondas. And they built a hull fleet o' boats, canoes an' all, for me, and had 'em ready to receive me. But when they seed me steerin' up to their port on my pet, a ninety-seven feet Missippy Crocodile, already harnessed for the expedition with my first mate, Ben Hardin, settin' on the ring o' the crittur's tail an' holdin the reins, while I sot on his back, cracked my twisted buffalo skin, and tickled old Mississippi under the fore legs to make him go, the authorities give ninety cheers and a hundred guns for Crockett and Ben Hardin. So off we started, a leetle faster than thinking, to find the t'other end o' thar longest river, Rio Medaria. An' we did it, measurin' and all, in six days. It war jist 2300 miles long. We killed an' skinned jist two hundred Auntycondas, and giv 'em to my Crocodile for feed; choked fifty tigers to death; an' tamed the yaller king o' Brazillian wild pusses till he was as docile as a new-born rabbit, brought him home, and presented him to my feller adventerer, Jimmy Raymond, the great Colonel o' menageries.

117

Crockett Taming a Panther

You hear a great talk and tin trumpeting about sartin brute tamers, sich as Carter Greaseback and the hull on 'em. They are very savagerous it's true; but arter all it takes me to teach them toothiferous beasts civilization, and eat a cat, as fashionables say. Why, I once made a buffalo so tame that he used to come to meetin every Sunday and roar the base o' the ole hundred without missin' a single note—and that same identical crittur would even lend the leader his horn for a tunin' fork. An' I once tamed a she-wolf at sich an all-civilized rate that one summer when I had the bone-rattlin' ague, she would come an' shake an' yawn for me; and of a clar night, the way she would look at the full moon and howl astronomy at me was astonishin to education—if it warn't then grind me up in a mill for tanbark.

One stormy mornin I took an airin' for about ten miles in the forest through a hailstorm, for to recover my appetite, and goin' for a mere walk of pleasure, I didn't take my thunder-bolt and execution knife along, and had nothing but a little club that I took to part the trees with. Having walked about eight miles my appetite begun to make my mouth wink. I believe I could have ground up a hickory stump, roots and all, so I longed for something to get at. Directly I happened to hold the lanthorn o' my peepers through a black thicket, an' I saw the two eyes of a squadruped crittur in the mouth of a cave, burning like a double jack-o-lanthorn; so I give a loud horse neigh of joy, kase I thought there war either sport or a breakfast ahead. I darted into the lane of the cave over bones and skulls as thick as pumpkins in a patch, an' next moment I stood within three paces of a strappin' he-panther, settin upon the root of his tail, and grinnin' at the bare bones as if he war about twice as hungry as I was.

He licked his teeth and growled; I grated thunder with mine, signifying that one of us war to be eaten up an' no mistake. We showed nails an' tusks, and looked eye lightnin at one another for some time, in which he gave me to understand that he was the terror an' big eater o' the forest, and that his teeth

118

war o' the crosscut saw disposition, an' his stomach a forty stone mill, an' that he would make a ghost of me instantaneously.

I grinned a sixty power sawmill at him. Says I, "I'm Davy Crockett, an' tarnacious hungry, which means teetotalacious devourish to any warm-blooded squadruped." For a half dozen o' his wildpuss nation war nothing more than a stomach stayer for me; an' I begun gnawin' my club till the fire flew at every crack o' my tusks.

He then give three or four sweeps with his tail, and a canterin' yell that was equal to about twenty manpower, an' we both advanced, givin' a growl an' gratin' our teeth mutually hostilacious, our eyes shootin' horrid, an' blazin' white fire like dead lightnin afore a gust breaks out. Another growl brought us tight together, tugging for death or breakfast; his claws walked into my shoulder savagerously impertinent. I put my tusks into his front parts till his bones creaked, and the way the wind carried the fur about was equal to Sampson and the lion. He was about makin' a choice chop of my left cheek, when I gin him an upward blow under the jaw, and a gouger in the bread-trough, that brought him over on his back, yelpin' for marcy.

So I jist took him by the curl of the tail, and raising my little forest wand, taught him all sorts o' civilization; made him put up his paws and say his prayers, and howl the tenor of a psalm—till, having made him a perfect penitent, I drove him home afore me, and astonished the natives with a converted panther. If I didn't, then saw me up for weather boards.

An' that same animal has ever since been a screamin' pet o' mine. When I come home of a dark nite, he'll light me up to bed with the fire of his lookers; he brushes the hearth off every mornin with his tail, an' o' Saturdays does all my wife's heavy work. He rakes in all her garden seed with his claws, does all of little Buffalo Crockett's extra screamin', wipes our feet off with his back arter we wash 'em, helps to currycomb the horses with his nails, and lets my wife hackle flax upon his teeth. If he don't, then feed me for dinner to a flock o' hungry wildcats in winter.

Crockett at Home

Thar's no human flesh in all creation that's so partial to home and the family circle, square, kitchen, barn, log-hut, pig-pen or fire-place as a Kentuckian. For my own part, I war in the habit, every mornin', of lightin' my pipe, and givin' all my domestic circle — wimmin, colts, wild cats, and kittens — an all-squeezin' hug all round; and the way the brute portion of 'em showed thar sharp ivories, and grinned back double extra satisfaction, war indeed upwards of gratifying to my mortal and sympathetic natur. But you see, while I war abroad in Texas an' Mexico, I war of course teetotally deprived of all these trimmins, an' it sort o' petrified an' soured my cream of human kindness, an' I felt jist about as solitary as a single corpse in a country church-yard. An' so for fear I mought ketch the common civilized complaint called Miss-ann-throw-py, an' knowing that thar war no dependable human natur in the Mexican people, I detarmined to go out an' tame myself a family circle o' wild cats an' bears.

Now, you must be fully aware of the fact, that the wild beasts of Mexico have nat'rally more ferocity — more never-to-be-tamed-ness an' thunder-bolt disposition — than all other walkin' and creepin' things.

However, when I take up a notion to put any thing through, nothin' stops me — nothin'! So out I travelled into a dark den of about six hundred acres, called "Devouration Swamp"— an' by the stars in Miss Uncle Sam's striped petticoat — thar I lit upon the most tarrificacious natural menagerie and zoological collection of critturs that ever skeered the skies out of their blue complexion. The snakes spit blue and red lightnin' at me, the big bears growled all sorts o' low thunder, the wolves howled all sorts o' north-east hurrycanes, while the panthers an' Mexican tigers screamed loud enough to set an edge on the teeth of a mill-saw. But all this 'ere only stepped up my courage an' desire to jump into 'em, and I licked the whole den of varmints so that they come and licked my hands in the most prostrate position — and they have formed my family circle ever since.

PEDLARS AND PUKES

A Puke

Of all the ticklar geniuses from Uncle Sam's twenty-six states, the Pukes, as we'll call 'em, are the most all-sickenin' ugly critters that the wet Western land can breed an' turn out. Now I boast of being too ugly to get out of bed arter sunrise, myself, for fear I'd scare him back again, but then I ain't sickly ugly; the Puke is so etarnally so, that his own shadow always keeps behind him, for fear that his all-spewy lookin' face would make it throw itself up. The Pukes never look each other in the face but once a year, an' that's in the spring, when they want to vomit off their surplus bile.

I once hired one to work in my mill, but the tarnal walking emetic no sooner looked at a hopper than he turned its stomach, and set the stones goin' round in double speed, and the hopper got so sick that it threwed up grist stones and all — if he didn't, grind me up for buffalo feed. If you are a business man, never you settle in the Puke state, for they'll make you throw up vittals, business and all — if they don't, cut me up for vomits.

A Hoosier

Now the Hoosiers are a different class o' human natur altogether. They are half taller an' bristles, an' so all-sweaten fat and round, that when they go to bed they roll about like a cider barrel in a cellar, an' therefor they're always obleeged to have a nigger each side on 'em to keep 'em still; an' when they wake up, they have to fasten down their cheeks before they can open their eyes. A Hoosier can eat a hog, tail, fur and all, and in the fall of the year, the bristles come out on him so splendifferous thick that he has a regular nateral tippet about his throat, an' a nateral hogskin cap on his head. I once had one of these half-starved critters to work on my plantation — till one hot day come, and if he didn't spill his hull self, nails, hair and all, into my hay wagon, then cut me up for shoe greasers; an' arter we cooled it, thar he was a complete cake o' hog fat, an' thar was enough on him to grease all the harnesses and wagons for a hull year.

A Sucker

Of all human fish, big fish, and little fish, your regular Sucker is the etarnalist oddest fish I ever put my upper story lights upon. His whole life is a regular suck-in. Now I can swoller a Lake Su-
perior o' lightnin water, meanin' whiskey, in a superior fashion — but when I do, it lasts me till I git dry again; but a Sucker never takes time to git dry, for he hangs to a bottle like a buzzard to a hoss bone, an' if he ever lets go, it's because his tarnal legs let go of his body. The suckin' straw drools about between his lips, his body lets go of itself, an' down he rolls like a tilted rum barrel, till his stomach turns a regular somer-set, and his spirit runs out o' the great gape or bung hole in his face, like water through the flood gate of a mill dam. And when his red beet of a nose gets into it, thar's a boiling an' steamification that rolls up sich an all-sickening smell that you begin to see spots on the sun, and swar that he's getting the small pox.

A Wolverine

The chaps from the Wolverine state are the all-greediest, ugliest, and sourest characters on all Uncle Sam's twenty-six farms. They are, in thar natur, like their wolfish namesakes, always so etarnal hungry that they bite at the air, and hang their underlips, and show the harrow teeth of their mouths, as if they'd jump right into you, and swaller you hull, without salt. They are, in fact, half wolf, half man, and tother half saw mill. I met a Wolverine one day in the forest, who had just swallowed a buck, an' that war only enough to start his appetite, an' make him all-ravenous; he turned up his eyes at me, an' opened his arthquake jaws as if he war goin to chop off my head without axin'. I chucked a lamb or two at him, but it war no more use than a hoss-fly to a buzzard.

"Mr. Wolverine," says I, "you stare at me with a reg'lar cannibal grin, but darn me, if you mustn't fight before you can bite; my name's Crockett, and I'm an airthquake."

And if the critter didn't draw up his under-lip, and fall to eating off the bark of a tree, while his eyes watered along with his mouth, then take my whiskers for wolf skins.

Heavy Timbered Land

"Is the land well timbered?" inquired a person of a Wolverine who was offering a tract of land for sale. "I vum," replied the vender, "it is a most almighty piece of land, and so heavy timbered that a humming bird could not fly through it. As I was passing upon the road along side of it tother evening, I heard a loud cracking and crashing in the trees, so I looked to see what it was, and I'm darned if it were not the moon trying to get through the branches but 'twas so tarnation thick she couldn't do it, so down she went, and I had to go home in the dark."

A Corncracker's Encounter
with an Eelskin

Of all the cursed Adam varmints in creation, keep me clear of a Yankee pedlar. They swarm the whole valley of the Mississippi, with their pewter watches and horn gun flints, peppermint drops and essences. Although the greatest chaps in creation for brag and sarce, they always play possum when there is danger, and skulk out the back door over the fence in no time. With their ribbons and dashy trash they are able to make love to the gals with every advantage over the real natives.

I was once courting a fine little gal on Swamp Creek, in Old Kaintuck. I went once a fortnight as she lived twenty miles off. One day I took my rifle and cut out for bears. Having taken the direction of her house, I got so near it that I determined to make a call on my doxy. On arriving at the house and opening the door what should I see but my little gal sitting in the lap of a tarnal pedlar. The little jade as soon as she saw me jumped out of his lap, blushing like a red cabbage. I looked fierce and the feller looked as slunk in the face as a baked apple.

Said I, "Stranger, do you make purtensions to this gal; what are you?"

"I'm first rate and a half and a leetle past common. I can blow through a pumpkin vine and play on a cornstalk fiddle with any man, and whittle the leetle eend of a stick to nothing. But mister, you havn't seen nothing of no horse with crop ears and a switch tail in the woods, ain't ye? I lost a sleek two year old mare in the woods yesterday."

Said I, "Stranger, you are a damn red eel: and if you ain't off in no time, I'll take off my neckcloth and swallow you whole."

He had a basket of essence vials on the floor. I gave it sich a kick that the vials flew about most beautiful. The fellow now found it was time to be off, and if my gal hadn't interfeared, I was so wrothy I should have scun him alive. Arter the critter was off I looked glum enuff, but the little varmint come and sat down in my lap and put her arms round my neck and gave me a sweet buss, so I got over the huff directly.

126

Gum Swamp Breeding

The most unpolite trick that ever was done up in Gum Swamp, tho that is the most unpolite place inside of the Massissippy, was done when I was playing possum for a gal in my young days, before I had ever heered of Congress.

This gal was named Jerusha Stubbs, and had only one eye, but that was pritty enough for two, and besides it had a great advantage in our parts, where folks must rise early, as she could wake up in half the time that others could, as she had only one eye to open, while other folks had to open two. One of her legs was a little shorter than the other, but I telled her I shouldn't make no fuss about that as the road to my house laid all along on the side of a hill, so that the short leg seemed as if 'twas made a purpose for walking to my cabin. She had had two cancers cut out of her breast, so that she was as flat as a board up and down there, which I couldn't have got over no how, only she had a beautiful great hump on her back, and that made up for having nothing of the kind in front. Enermost all her teeth had rotted out, but then she had a pesky great swallow, so that she could take down her vittles without chawing. I forgot to say how she had a hare-lip, but then she had a long nose, which almost covered the place from sight. There was a great bunch on her left arm, but then she had a monstracious wen on the right side of her neck, that balanced that difficulty and made it all even agin. She was wonderful neat at pulling up parsnips, and could shake a dog by the ears, and they did tell how she chased one till his tail drew out and war left behind. She could lick two foxes, and make a wolf feel pesky unsartin. She once busted a pair of bellusses by blowing in at the nose of 'em, and smothered a chimney that war on fire by setting on the top of it.

You may suppose such a gal as that would be scarce in courting, for she could put a hole through any man's heart at seventy paces distance. Onluckily I warn't on very good terms with her father, tho he war with me. So I got acquainted with the gal a leetle at a time. I knowed her pritty well from her shoulders and upwards, but she kept her mind to herself, and that made me feel as oneasy as a steamboat with one wheel.

But I felt hugeously mad, when a feller from down east come into Gum Swamp, and put up at her father's house with all his plunder. He was a school-master, and tho I say it myself, he was kind of good looking and as slick as an eel standing up on his tail. I sot and lookt on whilst he was talking to the gal, and didn't know what to do about it for a good while; but when I begun to git over not knowing what to do about it, I felt an almighty notion to shove my thum nail into his left eye. Jerusha seed I was getting to be very odoriferous about it, tho a word from her would have laid my bristles in a minnit.

At last she sot down to table one day, with her good eye next to the stranger, and her blind eye next to me. I took that for the most onrespectful thing that was ever done to me, and looked rite at the stranger, as if I war thinking whether it war best to swallow him or the dinner. You might as well try to play a game of cards on the back of a running deer, as to give a picter of how he looked. I can't rightly say how many colors he turned, but I know I seed three or four colors in his face that I never seed ennywhere else. I've heered tell of fellers that felt blue, but he felt all colors, besides a spot on the eend of his nose.

So he axed me what I was grinning at, and I says, says I, "Stranger, I don't want to onsult you before the gal, but if I had you in the forest I'd hang you on the limb of a tree by your onquestionably ugly nose."

He then axed his gal if it would be imperlite if he jist took the tip of my nose between his thum and finger and give it a small pull. He told her he would do nothing more, and would make no noise about it, and that he could do it all in half a minnit. She told him he might do that if he chooze, but she wouldn't allow onnything else to be done about it, only that; and so she leaned back in her cheer, to let him put his arm out before her, and do what he said.

That was the fust time I was so mad I couldn't stir, to think the cussed varmint should talk of pulling my nose as if it was only snuffing a candle that couldn't strike back again.

128

I was thinking whether I should eat him with salt, or take
him in his boots jist as he was, when I seed him lay down his
knife and fork and reach out his hand. I sot as still as a clam till
he got his hand close to my mouth, and then I opened shell and
took his flipper between my teeth. He yelled like a nest of
young wildcats struck with litening, and insinewated it hurt
him beautiful. The gal begun to bawl out and take the feller's
part, and that astonished me so much that I forgot to let go the
feller's hand till my teeth almost met through it. There was a
smart chance of hot soup on the table, and that was kicked over

129

rite off, for he floundered about like a speared salmon, without stopping this time to ax the gal whether it would be imperlite or not. She ketched hold of his coat tail to haul him away from me, but that only hurt him wuss, and so to git clear of her he kicked backwards, and put his heels into her bowels like he was going to walk over her. Pritty soon the hot soup begun to run down into his boots, and he danced wuss than ever and upset the table, and all the dishes went to smash. At last he got on his knees and axed my pardon, and then I let him go.

Now I went home and thot it was all over, but what does the gal's father do but send me a bill for the crockery, that the feller broke when he upsot the table. I thot this was the most unpolite thing that ever I heered on, and so I sent the money bekase it would be a disgrace to me for sich a mean feller to think I owed him anything.

The Pedlar's Fright

Jist before the frost come, one fall, a long-legged cream-faced Yankee pedlar brought his plunder into the forest, for to tice our gals out of their munny. He put up for a time with a feller called Flunky Bill, who lived in a log cabin on the edge of Skunk's Paradise. This pedlar war most abominable on-scrupulous in his dealings, and knowed no more about han-dling a rifle than a goose knows about rib stockings; but he borrowed a rifle one arternoon, and went out into the woods to kill some varmints. He didn't come back that nite, and Flunkey sot up for him and kept a pine knot burning half the nite. And the way he didn't come home all the nixt day was a caution. So Bill didn't know but what something had happent to the pesky critter, and he raised the nabors to go and hunt arter him. I should a thort he had run away on purpus, only he left his plunder behind, and I knowed very well he wouldn't do that if he didn't expect to come back.

We went a day's journey into the forest, and kept a lookout on every hand; but we seed nothing of the pedlar. So when it begun to grow dark, we kindled a fire, and sot down and took out the whiskey. As soon as the fire began to burn well, we heered a sort of groaning noise, and as the fire war made under the branches of a big tree, we looked up, and my eyes, reader!, thar we seed a pair of long legs dangling down in the smoke, and they twisted and writhed like frying an eel alive!

So we begun to scatter the fire, and Flunkey Bill bawled out, "There's the pedlar's legs — I should know them from a thousand."

True enuff, it war the pedlar, and we helped him down from the tree. When he got down he looked around him half fritened to death, till he seed Flunkey Bill, and then he knowed he war safe. The coward varmint told us he had been up in that tree nite and day, ever sence he left the cabin. He had seed a big snapping turtle that had come out of a pond close by, and he thort it war a alligator. So he had clum up into the tree, and if we hadn't a come, he would have staid up thar till he rotted. The pesky critter wanted to know, if he war safe arter he come down.

Ses I, "You are along with Davy Crockett, who is part snapping turtle himself, and a piece of the alligator; so if you are afeered of them varmints you had better git up in the tree agin."

Arter we got home, the gals got hold of the story, and the pedlar cleered out pretty quick, for they used to shove a turtle in his face whenever he wanted to sell 'em ennything.

Buy Log - Buy Nigger

When Phineas Dowdy war going to build him a new house, he got a passel of logs from Sam Davis. When they got the logs home, they found one of 'em had been a holler tree, and they thort they wood split it open to make rails of. As soon as they had put in the wedges and used the beetle a few, it come open very slick, and what do you think war inside of it? A pesky great bull nigger. Some of the chaps knowed him. It war Davis's nigger that had run away and hid in a holler tree, and when the tree was cut down, he didn't know enuff to crawl. Now you must know that Phineas had bort the logs and paid for 'em; but as soon as Davis had heerd that his nigger war found, he come arter him.

Sez he, "Phineas, have you got my nigger?"

Phineas opened his mouth, and showed all his teeth, for a beginning, and then he sez, "I've got nothin but what I bort of ye — for the logs war paid for, and I hope you haint come for to begin any arterclaps."

"A nigger's a nigger, and logs is logs," sez Davis, "and when you wants niggers, you must buy niggers; and when you wants logs you must buy logs."

Then Phineas begun to move his ears, and his left eye struck out like a unicorn's horn, and he axed Davis if he meant to insinewate anything disrespectable agin his honesty. Davis war a little man, and when he seed Phineas was riz, his skin crawled, and he marched off.

But Davis war on the trail, and meant to be paid for his nigger. So at the nixt 'lection, he seed an old nag belonging to Phineas, and a fine nigger named Sam war riding him. He axed Phineas how much he would ax him for the hoss, and Phineas said he would take fifteen dollars. So the bargain war struck, and Davis jumpt up behind the nigger and put the hoss on the wild trot. Phineas run arter 'em, but it war like swimming arter a steambote. On the nixt day, Phineas went arter his nigger, but Davis told him he bort the hoss, and if thar war a nigger on him, it war like the nigger in the holler log.

Then Phineas seed he war chawed up, and he didn't know what to say. He war going to law about it, but I told him he had better keep still, for it war a bad rule wot wouldn't work two ways at wunst. So he squat low and sung dumb; but he would be as mad and riprocious as a turtle without a shell whenever ennybody said ennything to him arterward about "buy log — buy nigger."

132

A Miracle

Thar are some rogues who are very slick, and thar are some who are as blind as a mole. Thar war one feller that lived away east, and he set up for a profit,* and got away a good deal of the peeple's munny. He had a great menny to follow him, and he purtended to larn 'em things what never war and never will be agin. At last, he telled 'em he would do a mirikle. He got about twenty of the softest of 'em to make a journey with him into the forest, for he purtended he couldn't work a mirikle where thar war so many disbeleevers. So they followed him about two hundred mile, and at last he come to the banks of the Massissippy, and I happened to be out thar with my rifle. I seed a passel of strangers, and hurried up to 'em.

Then the profit put on a long face and stept towards me. I didn't like his looks, for he had a sheepish eye, and drawed up his mouth, more like a rogue than a fool. He war half and half, like a mulatter nigger. He war foolish enuff to come a-near Davy Crockett, even tho he war too cunning for them as he brot with him on his fools errant.

So I sallied up to 'em, and sez I, "Strangers, how faree? Glad to see ye, I'm Davy Crockett, known all over the world, and ye're welcome to the forest. It's none of my bizness to ax your bizness here, but as you must be dry a-walkin', here's a jug of whisky and my cabin is not fur off, whar we can fill it when it's empty."

When the profit heered my speech, he looked as gloomiriferous as a death's head, and drawn down his under lip as if his chin war loaded with lead. His company didn't dast to take a drop of the whiskey, and one of 'em spoke out, and sez he, "This is a holy man, who has come on a pilgrimidge, and we are his disciples, and are come on sacred bizness."

"Now, arnt that a good un," sez I, "I didn't come hear to pry into your business, like a fox smelling a hen roost, but I come to ax ye to moisten yer clay, and bid ye welcome."

They all turned off like a herd of buffaloes, and begun to

*Prophet.

133

listen to thar preacher. He set to praying like a steembote, and presently he begun to speak about faith, and said he would remove mountains or turn the water up stream. Then he stood still a minnit, and lookt very suspishus at me, but he begun his mirikle. "You see yon log," sez he, and he pinted to a pesky great alligator that laid up on the shore in the sun, a little ways off, so he lookt like a log whar we stood. They all lookt at it, and then sez he, "Now, by faith I will remove that log into the deep. It shall skip like a ram, at the word of the Lord." So he walked along toward the alligator, and flung a stone at him, when the cretur usked up, and run into the water. His followers tumbled down on thar knees as if they had been shot, and begun to worship the profit.

I run up to 'em and sez I, "You dratted fools, did you never see a crockadile run afore?"

With that the profit come rite up to me, and lookt in my face, with his big black eyes, as if he would skeer me out of my common cents, and said, "Thou blasfemer, depart; for behold a mighty mirikle has now been performed, before all the people. Depart, you onbeleeving Farisee!"

I war struck dumb at the feller's impudence; but my blood war all a-biling, and I itched to have my fingers in his hair.

"Now," sez I, "you monstracious great hypocrit, you oncivil, lying, pestiliferous vagrandizing scorpion, I'll tell you what it is. You are a stranger, and so I won't be oncivil to you — but if you tell me that that ar thing that you called a log war not a crockodile, I say you are a lying son of a gun."

Then the sarpunt turned round to his peeple, and sez he, "Lay hold on him, in the fear of the Lord, and cast him into the great waters."

I jist stept back one pace, and raised my rifle, and drew a lead on their profit. Then sez I, "Now, let's see one of ye lay a hand on David Crockett, and see how soon I'll drop the Lord's anointed by putting a ball thro' his holiness's gizzard."

When they seed their profit war in danger, they dasn't stir an inch, but if I had aimed at them they would have come at his word of command like John Bull's bullies when they marched up to the breastwork in New Orleans.

The profit begun to look wonderiferous and he turned white as love in his face; and then he turned round, and said he shook the dust of Kentucky off his feet, and they all cleared out as swift as they could bundle. I hollered arter him, and told him the dust of old Kaintuck would come off his feet without shaking, for it wouldn't cleave to his ugly onmentionable corpse, any more than my dog Tupe would cling to a skunk. None on us ever seed anything of the humbug arter that: — and no profits ever come into our parts since that ar time.

Simon Shadbrim The Quaker

A rig'lar Quaker is a leetle bit the deceivenist critter in all natur, and more sly than a 'possum in a consumption. Going home one day about dusk, I run agin something, but as I couldn't see anything of more substance than a piece o' damp nothing, I concluded it must be a bit of grey twilight, streaking home afore dark. But, taking a step farther, I found it war the leanest kind of a Quaker, holding his breath to save his lungs, and walking light to save his shoes.

The all-staggerinist deception of this sort I ever experienced was one cloudy day, when I was walking across old Simon Shadbrim's cornfield. I started a fine flock o' ducks, so I lifted old Thunderbolt and follered. Seeing they didn't mind the fox-feather in my skull, I jist bent horizonticklar-like, and was in a clean way for taming 'em to enter death by distributin' my saltpetre upon their tails, when rather suddenaciously my peepers lit right upon the wings of a riglar dark blue buzzard, spreading out about as elegant as the arms of a big black oak.

Now I hold the spite of a hull sawmill agin these feathered an' flyin' re-surrectionists — they're in particklar 'bad odour' with me, and I'd rather pick one on 'em out of creation than shoot a bag o' the best game in Kentuck. So I jist weaseled a

135

leetle nigher an' nigher, pointed old Thunderbolt, taking clar aim right at his foul stomach, and was jist about on the tip eend o' blowin' the critter into the water, bad smell and all, when I thought I smelt somethin drabbish. I stept a leetle further, and by all shy critters, if thar didn't stand old Simon Shadbrim in the character of a scarecrow, with a barrack roof of a hat that I took for a buzzard wing.

"Umph," says he.

"Umph," says I. "Old Shaddy, if I warn't nigh making buzzard's vittals out o' you, take my nails for your tarnal drab coat buttons."

Advice to Strangers

The reeder needn't be skeered about coming into Old Kaintuck, no how. We aint a sarcumstance to the Injuns; but we are purty particklar about some things. We consider a feller a flunk and a sneak if he don't take an eye-opener in the morning and an antifogmatic about nine o'clock. He must always evapperate a horn full of whiskey when he's axed to do it, and he must stand up to his lick log on all occasions. If a man spits in his face, he is duty bound to say something about it; but if he gits knocked down, that's his own bizziness, for its very different from an insult. If he can't hunt, perhaps he can fight; and if he can't fight perhaps he can scream; and if he can't scream, perhaps he can grin pretty severe; and if he can't do that, perhaps he can tell a story.

We always expect something of a stranger; but we shan't stand crockodile mirikles, nor encourage cowardly pedlars, nor any other pesky varmints in our cleering.

A Pedlar Disguised

Them Yankees from down East is the most pestiferous set of varmints that ever came into old Kaintuck. Thar war a Yankee pedlar that had been round our clearing for some time, and war arter a darter of Pine Wing. He squinted with one eye, and the other kept looking up for rain. So she keered about him, and war in a great flustification to go a-shopping at the place where he was, and buy her a saddle horse.

The gal war never no judge of the article, though she could tell a bear from a panther by the feel of his bite, when it war so dark that she couldn't hear herself talk. The hoss was lame in his fore legs, and in his hind legs too, and he had a crook in his tail. He was blind of one eye and deaf of both ears. He couldn't stand up, he was so infirm, and he couldn't lay down because his bowels were out of order. So Pine Wing told the hoss-jockey that if he didn't make tracks, he'd skin him alive.

He went off, and in about a week arterwards, a pesky injin come to the cabin, and pertended to be catawampously tired, and wanted a supper. Pine was always as free as a sap maple, and he rolled out the whiskey barrel to him, and told him to drink out of the bung. But when the cretur stooped down to drink, a mask fell off, and showed the weazen'd sallow chops of the infarnal pedlar.

137

With that, Pine Wing jumped up, and screamed like a paint-er. Then he lit on the pedlar, who fell on his knees and squawked like a strangling goose. Pine axed him whether he would choose to lose an eye or an ear. He begged to lose nary one, and said he would do anything,— he would lick up the dust, or be a slave all his life, if he could be spared. Then Pine drew off, and give him a kick that sent him through the window, and said he war too cussed mean to be shot, and that he war too light to be hung, as thar wasn't meat enough on his bones to stretch his neck. He cleared out and war never heered of arterwards.

A Missourian's Opinion of His Neighbor

Jedediah Crawfish was very fond of his neighbor's wife, and went with his friend Elnathan to see her one afternoon. Jede-diah went up stairs and left Elnathan below to watch. Pres-ently the husband came home, and greeted Elnathan cordially. He told him that he had long suspected Jedediah of improper tenderness towards his wife, and said, "As you are his intimate friend, you may tell me whether you think he is guilty."

"I have known my friend Crawfish for twenty years," re-plied Elnathan, "and would not be afraid to stake my head that he is above doing a bad action."

Crockett on the Oregon Question

I expose the reader has heered o' them diggins out West, that are called Oregon, and how the British wants to have a joint occupacy of that 'ere clearing. It's a sort of insinewation that we can't take keer of it alone, and it puts me in mind o' the joint occupacy of me and a painter when we both found our-selves together on a branch of a tree. The place war big enough for us both, but we couldn't agree to stay there together.

Thar war once a pesky Yankee pedlar that put up at my house, and had as much bear's meat and whiskey in his long guts as he could carry, but he wasn't satisfied with that, for he wanted the joint occupacy of my wife too. So when I got out of bed early in the morning, he crept along to the disputed territory and began to turn down the coverlid. My wife heered him, and made believe she war asleep, but kept one eye open. Jest as he put one leg into bed, she took a clothesline that hung close by, an' tied it round his ankle, and made him fast by one leg to the bed-post. Then she got up and opened a hive of bees on him. He danced and roared most beautiful. And I think John Bull will do the same when he gits among the Yankee bees of Oregon.

A Methodizer Saving Souls

I war riding to St. Louy one day in the year six, with a richus buck on each side of my hoss, for I'd been bouncing deer on Tantivy prairie. I kinder thort I'd let my hoss have a mouthful out of the Mississip, when I heerd a most riproarious hollering, as if fifty thousand devils were having their tails chopped off close to their butt eends all at once and then having the hoperation gone over agin closer.

So thinking it war two painters fiteing, I looked sharp at my priming and rode that way, expecting to get a shot and maybe two. But when I got thar I wish I may be shot if it war not a Methody parson a-whaling it into the natives to kill. The brute war enticing 'em all to kingdom come by a short cut he had found out, he said, and the way he explaterated to 'em war a caution. Thar war one feller streaking it up to the pulpit on his knees, enough to make his wife sneeze her nose off, if she had the mending on 'em. Then thar war a feller two foot longer than the moral law galravaging on a stump and trying to reach Heaven, he said. I told him he'd better go atop of the next bluff, but he took no notice of me, and another feller told me to shut up my saltbox for fear the flies should get down my

throat. The gals war all a crying and that made me feel quite solumkolly. But what made me the maddest was to see as many as a hundred niggers turning up the whites of their eyes, jest as if they had soles to be saved. "If I war to ketch you galli-wanting so on my plantation, mister," sez I to myself, "I'd make an American flag of your back in the twinkling of a bed-post." However, the parson got done soon, and marched rite down into the Mississip, and hauled two or three niggers in after him, and ducked them so often that I thought the life was extincti-fied in 'em.

Bimeby up comes a puke from Wheatbush more than half and half absquottleated with licker, and sez he, "I say, mister, what do you get apiece for washing them ar niggers?"

Well, if the Methodizer war not mad then there's no snakes in Virginny, and he as good as told him he war a viper or a copperhead, I disremember which.

The other feller wouldn't say the hard word for all that. "You needn't come for to go to be so cantankerous about it, stranger," sez he, "for I meant to give you a job. I've got a couple of little niggers at hum, and if you can wash 'em white I wouldn't mind paying you something hansum and a chaw of tobacco."

And he got so atrocious that if somebody hadn't held him he'd have walked into the Methodizer knee deep, and a foot deeper.

I was so kynd of curous to see what war going on that I went down to the edge of the water, jest as the Methodizer laid his cornstealers on a wench blacker than the ace of spades, and fatter than a December bear, and led her up to the neck into the drink. Down he shoved her wooly calabash under water and up popped her starn, bekayse any fool mought know it's nateral for grease to float. The Methodizer was discomboborated a few and shoved her starn down agin, and then up shot her topknot. He couldn't git her whole corporosity under no how he could fix it, till he hauled her in whar she couldn't touch bottom; then the current took her bodily, and the Methodizer would have gone down stream with her like a Pawnee with another man's hoss if he hadn't let her go, and she'd swallowed so much water

141

already that she evaporated like steam. The Methodizer didn't seem to mind it no more than if she didn't cost nothing.

"There's one gone to thy kingdom!" sez he, "fetch me another. Won't you come to glory, mister, won't you come?"

"No," sez I, "I thank you as kyindly as if I did, but I can't swim."

A Bundling Match

When I was a big boy that had jist begun to go a-galling, I got astray in the woods one arternoon; and being wandering about a good deal and got pretty considerable soaked by a grist of rain, I sot down on to a stump and begun to wring out my leggins, and shake the drops off of my raccoon cap. Whilst I was on the stump I got kind of sleepy, and so laid my head back in the crotch of a young tree that growed behind me, and shot up my eyes. I had laid out of doors for many a night before with a sky blanket over me — so I got to sleep pretty soon and fell to snoring most beautiful. So somehow or somehow else I did not wake till near sundown, and I don't know when I should have waked had it not been for somebody tugging at my hair. As soon as I felt this, though I wan't more than half awake, I begun to feel to see if my thum nail was on, as that was all the ammunition I had about me. I lay still to see what the feller would be at. The first idee that I had was that a cussed Injun was fixing to take off my scalp, so I thought I'd wait till I begun to feel the pint of his knife scraping against the skin, and then I should have full proof agin him, and could jerk out his copper-colored liver with all the law on my side. At last I felt such a hard twist that I roared right out, but when I found that my head was squeezed so tight in the crotch that I could not get it out, I felt like a gone sucker. I felt raal ridiculous I can assure you; so I begun to talk to the varmint and told him to help me get my head out, like a man, and I would give him five dollars before I killed him. At last my hair begun to come out by the roots, and then I was mad to be took advantage of in that way. I swore at the varmint till the tree shed all its leaves and the sky turned yaller. So in a few minutes I heerd a voice, and then a gal come running up and axed what was the matter. She soon saw what was to pay, and told me that the eagles were tearing out my hair to build nests with. I told her that I had endured more han a dead possum could stand already, and that if she would drive off the eagles I would make her a present of an iron comb.

"That I will," says she, "for I am a she steamboat and have doubled up a crocodile in my day."

So she pulled up a small sapling by the roots, and went to work as if she hadn't another minnit to live. She knocked down two of the varmints, and screamed the rest out of sight. Then I telled her the predicament I was in, and she said she would loosen the hold that the crotch had on my head. Up she went into the tree, and spanned her legs over my head like a rainbow. She put one foot agin one side of the crotch, and the other foot agin tother, and pushed as hard as she could. I was always as modest as an unweaned calf, but I could not help looking up as my head was held in one position.

But I soon felt the limbs begin to loosen and then I jerked out my head. As soon as I was clear, I could not tell which way to look for the sun, and I was afeard I should fall into the sky, for I did not know which way was up, and which way was down. Then I looked at the gal that had got me loose. She was a strapper. She was as tall as a sapling, and had an arm like a keelboat's tiller. So I looked at her like all wrath, and as she come down from the tree, I says to her, "I wish I may be utterly onswoggled if I don't know how to hate an injun or love a gal as well as any he this side of Roaring River. I fell in love with three gals at once at a log rolling, and as for tea squalls, my heart has never shut pan for a minnit at a time; so if you will bundle with me to-night, I will forgive the tree and the eagles for your sake!"

Then she turned white as an egg-shell, and I seed that her heart was busting, and I run up to her, like a squirrel to his hole, and gave her a buss that sounded louder than a musket. So her spunk was all gone, and she took my arm as tame as a pigeon, and we cut out for her father's house. We hadn't gone fur before one of her garters come off, but she soon made up for that by taking a rattling snake from his nest, and having knocked out his brains agin a stone, she wound him around her leg as brisk as a Yankee pedlar would tie up his budget. She told me that her Sunday bonnet was a hornet's nest garnished with wolves' tails and eagles' feathers, and that she wore a bran new gown

147

made of a whole bear's hide, the tail sarving for a train. She said she could drink of the branch without a cup, could shoot a wild goose flying, and wade the Mississippi without wetting her shift. She said she could not play on the piano nor sing like a nightingale, but she could outscream a catamount and jump over her own shadow; she had good strong horse sense and knew a woodchuck from a skunk. So I was pleased with her, and offered her all my plunder if she would let me split the difference and call her Mrs. Crockett.

She said she would try bundling fust, and that she must insult her father before she could go so fur as to marry. So I shut pan and sung dumb till we got to the house. We went into a room where there was a bed, and by this time it was quite dark. She consented to haul off all but her under petticoat and so I thought I had a fine bargain. But I soon found my mistake. Her under petticoat was made of briar bushes woven together, and I could not come near her without getting stung most ridiculous. I would as soon have embraced a hedgehog. So I made an excuse to go out, and then I cut through the bushes like a pint of whiskey among forty men. I never went that way since.

Col. Crockett in the Parlor

When I first went to take a squint at Kurnel Korpussle I some expected to see a grand place, something like our court house, but that wasn't the smallest part of a circumstance to it. My eyes, if there wan't a looking glass in it Jemmy Tweed might a seen himself in from the buck tail in his hat to his shoe sole, and he's the tallest man in all Kentuck; but I can whip him though. It was all sot in solid gold. The Kurnel was as perlight as all outdoors, and ses he, "How do you kyind a sorter find yourself, Crockett?" Then he axed me to smoke a segar, and I thanked him I would, but it was warm enough to roast injuns, and I'd take a flem-cutter first. Then we sot down to smoke and talk over the affairs of the nation.

I was hugeously ashamed to spit on that splendiferous carpit, but there was no help for it, tho' he didn't kyind of seem to like it, nor the sarvunt neither. Howzever, the nigger come in with a little tin box with a leetle hole in the top of it, and sot it down rite where I'd been spitting. It are a fact it wur painted all over with flowers so scientifically I thought there war something to eat in it, so I turned round and spit on the other side of my cheer. When the nigger saw that he come and put the box where I'd spit, and I had to turn round agin. And what do you think he done? Why, he put the box afore me once more, a purpose to set my bristles up. "I'll tell you what, Mr. Nigger," ses I, "it's well known I'm a peaceable man and I know better what belongs to good manners than to scalp you rite afore your master, but if you put that there box in my way agin I'll spit in it!"

Davy Crockett Losing His Speech

If ever I had my airthquake indignation riz to the double high pressure pinte, it war on my last tramp to take my seat in Congress. Now you see, I had jist rolled up and tied in an alligator's hide about fifty-four yards o' indignation speeches, on the state o' the nation. And, on my way through the Kentuck forest, I jist put the bundle at the root of the tree, while I cooked and killed a he-barr for my dinner. While I war crackin' the skull between my jaws, I heered a snortin' and scatterin' among the leaves; I jist revolved one o' my daylights around me, an' thar I seed a painter making off with my bundle o' patriotism an' Kentuck eloquence between his teeth. Well, not likin' to have my argument dijested by wildpuss bowels, I put arter him like a shootin' star scared by an airthquake, overtook the piratical varmint, split him in two with my life sarcher, carved his brains in with the butt eend of old Thunderbolt, captured my eloquence, an' swollered the entire puss instanter.

149

Colonel Crockett Delivering
His Celebrated Speech To Congress

ON THE STATE OF FINANCES, STATE OFFICERS,
AND STATE AFFAIRS IN GENERAL *

"Mr. Speaker:"

"The broken fenced state o' the nation, the broken banks,
broken hearts, and broken pledges o' my brother Congressmen here around me, has riz the boiler o' my indignation,
clar up to the high pressure pinte, an' therefore I have riz to let
off the steam of my hull hog patriotism, without round-about-
ation, and without the trimmins. The truth wants no trimmins,
for in her clar naked state o' natur she's as graceful as a suckin'
colt in the sunshine. Mr. Speaker! what in the name o' kill-
sheep-dog rascality is the country a-comin' to? Whar's all the
honor? no whar! an thar it'll stick! Whar's the state revenue?
every whar but whar it ought to be!

"Why, Mr. Speaker, don't squint with horror, when I tell
you that last Saturday mornin Uncle Sam hadn't the first fip
to give to the barber! the banks suspend payment, and the
starving people suspend themselves by ropes! old Currency is
flat on his back, the bankers have sunk all funds in the saft arth
o' speculation, and some o' these chaps grinnin' around me are
as deep in the mud as a heifer in a horse-pond!

"Whar's the political honesty o' my feller congressmen? why,
in bank bills and five acre speeches! Whar's all thar patriotism?
in slantendicular slurs, challenges, and hair trigger pistols!
Whar's all thar promises? every whar! Whar's all thar perform-
ances on 'em? no whar, and the poor people bellering arter 'em
everywhere like a drove o' buffaloes arter their lazy keepers,
that, like the officers here, care for no one's stomach, but their
own etarnal internals!

"What in the nation have you done this year? why, wasted

*In the panic year of 1837.

paper enough to calculate all your political sins upon, and that would take a sheet for each one o' you as long as the Mississippi, and as broad as all Kentucky. You've gone ahead in doin' nothin' backwards, till the hull nation's done up. You've spouted out a Mount Etny o' gas, chawed a hull Alleghany o' tobacco, spit a Niagary o' juice, told a hail storm o' lies, drunk a Lake Superior o' liquor, and all, as you say, for the good o' the nation; but I say, I swar, for her etarnal bankruptification.

"Tharfore, I move that the ony way to save the country is for the hull nest o' your political weasels to cut stick home instanterly, and leave me to work Uncle Sam's farm, till I restore it to its natural state o' cultivation, and shake off these state caterpillars o' corruption. Let black Dan Webster sittin there at the tother end o' the desk turn Methodist preacher; let Jack Calhoun settin right afore him with his hair brushed back in front like a huckleberry bush in a hurrycane, after Old Hickory's topknot, turn horse-jockey. Let Harry Clay sittin thar in the corner with his arms folded about his middle, like grape vines around a black oak, go back to our old Kentuck an' improve the breed o' lawyers an' other black sheep. Let old Daddy Quincy Adams sittin' right behind him thar, go home to Massachusetts, an' write political primers for the suckin' politicians; let Jim Buchanan go home to Pennsylvania, an' smoke long nine, with the Dutchmen. Let Tom Benton, bent like a hickory saplin with hall rolling, take a roll home an' make candy "mint drops" for the babies: — for they've worked Uncle Sam's farm with the all-scratching harrow o' rascality, 'till it's as gray as a stone fence, as barren as barked clay, and as poor as a turkey fed on gravel stones!

"And, to conclude, Mr. Speaker, the nation can no more go ahead under such a state o' things, than a fried eel can swim upon the steam o' a tea kettle; if it can, then take these yar legs for yar hall pillars."

Crockett Boiling a Dead Indian

One day, when my wife went out to a tea squall, she got into a holler tree out of the way of the rain; and while she war in thar she found a beautiful nest o' young bears. She put one into her bag, as she war sometimes lonesome when I war off hunting, and she had only fifteen cats, and wanted a bear by way of variety, as we sometimes take a glass of water instead of whiskey jest for a change. The bear stayed with us till he growed up, an' was always treated as one of the family. He used to set up to table with us, an' you ought to have seen the way he would put his paw into the soop an' feel all down to the bottom of the bowl to get hold of a bit of meat or a pertater.

But he took a bad cold one day on account of getting wet feet, an' I war obleeged to hunt up something delicate for the cretur as he had bad breath and showed symptoms of a bowel complaint. So I went out and shot an Injun, and sauced him up with little tender varmints, sich as toads, lizards, a crocodile's tail, and other spurious vegetables that was calculated to set well on a delicate stomack, and I biled 'em together, with directions to give the patient half a peck every two hours, and the bear got well directly.

A Receipt for the Cholera

Eat two cucumbers, dressed or raw, as you prefer; then take a quart of blackberries, four green corn, four young potatoes mashed, a lobster or a crab, some ice water, and wash the whole down with a quart of buttermilk, and you will shortly have a touch of the real thing.

Larned Courting

If the reader is had any experience, he ought to know as there are more kinds o' courting than one. One kind are where you shin up to a gal and give her a buss rite off, and take her by storm, as it wur; and then there are one kind whar you have a sneaking regard, and side up to her as if you war thinking about something else all the time, till you git a fair chance to nab her, and then you come out in good arnest. Thar are one kind whar you ax the gal's parents, and jine the church, and ar as steddy as a steembote, till arter marriage, when you may do as you like, seeing as how the game is run down.

But the greatest kind o' courting that ever I seed war the Larned Courting. It are a most beautiful thing for them as knows how, and I never had a try at it but wunst, and never want to agin; bekase it war so difficult to keep up my eend of the log.

Thar war a gal come into our parts when I war a young man, and lived on the little eend of little Salt Creek. She war very short in statue; but she war monstracious high in her notions, for she war always torking about the moon and the stars, and all them kind o' things what you cant touch with a ten foot pole. When she lit down in our parts, thar war a great stir among the young fellers, for she war fairer in the cheeks than our gals, and bekase she had sich little feet, so it wouldn't take much leather to keep her in shoes. Now I had an old dame living up in Carim Holler, and I thort it would be sort of ridiculous to go to see this gal. Her name war Kitty Cookins, and she lived within a rifle shot of my cabin; and my gal's name war Rueliana Drinkwater. Howsomever, I squatted low, and kept one corner of my eye open.

Thar war some almity ripsnorters that lived up near the south fork of Salt River, who war as broad between the two eyes as a New Orleans catfish; and when they smelt out Kitty, they rubbed up their coonskin breeches, and went down to see her. This put a kink into my idees at wunst, for I lookt at it as a sort of a stump, seeing as I lived closer to her than they did, and had the best right to set my trap for her. So I took Killdevil on my shoulder, one day, and sallied down to the Great Notch where she burrowed. When I got there I war all twisted up at sight of her, and didn't know which leg to put forward fust, for she war settin' on a green bank under a hemlock tree, dressed in a purty yaller frock, and had a book in her hand. She lookt up, and seed that I war in trouble, and she spoke rite out, and said "Good morning"; and when she showed her teeth, it war like two rows of mother pearl. I felt streaked all over, and would sooner have faced seven hungry painters in the forest; but twas too late to hang fire, and so I walked rite up to her.

Sez I, "How fare ye; I've heered that you war come into our clearing, and thort it would be no more nor naburly to cut out for your lodge, so here I be. Mebby you never heered of Davy Crockett, but come, its dry torking, and here is a bottle of whiskey."

I hope I may be shot if she didn't turn up her purty nose, and pout out her red lip at my whiskey, which you must know I took as a great insult, seeing it war the best whiskey in them parts. So I took twice as big a horn of it myself, as common, jist to be revenged, and then I sot down by the side of her. Then she begun to tork; but I don't know as I can give her exact lingo, for it war never heered in the forest before. She axed me if I war fond of reading, and I telled her that I had read the catekise when I war a child, and thort it only fit for children, but that I could draw a lead on a squirrel at three hundred paces, and swim the Massissippy blindfold, and double up any he this side of Roaring River.

She lookt down and begun to trot her little foot, and said thar war no defined people in the clearing, and how she inferred litter-a-toor and novelties, and loved to look at the moon, and the clouds, and how she liked cun-gineral sperits, and Sally Tude and vartue, and war going to cultivate bottiny and larn the use of yarbs. And then she read a little out of her book, and axed me if I war fond of poetness and duplicity. I telled her I didn't know about them kinds of varmints; but I liked a bear-steak, or a horn of mountain doo, and had drunk two sich fellers like her sweetheart onder in one evening.

Then she opened her big blue eyes and lookt at me so arnest, that I begun to think I had gin her a sort of a notion that she would like to stay with me, and so I war jist a going to put my arm round her neck, when I heered a noise in the bushes, and I ketched up old Killdevil, as I expected it war a painter. Purty soon I heered a squall; it sounded some like a painter, but it sounded more like my gal, Rueliana. I should know her squall from a hundred others, by moonlight, or in pitch dark mid-night. So I jumpt up from the place war I war setting, as I seed thar would be a breeze directly.

Rueliana broke ground through an elder bush, and come at me with her mouth wide open, and it scared the little gal Kitty so terrifficaciously that she run into the house and fastened the door; and it war well she did, or Ruey would have chawed her up like a wad, and wiped her teeth with the yaller frock. Then she flew at me like a mad alligator, and so I seed she loved me most horrid, and nobody ever dared to say Davy Crockett war ungrateful. So I never went to see the larned gal agin; but stuck to Ruey like a chestnut burr.

Davy Crockett's Dream

One day when it was so cold that I was afeared to open my mouth, lest I should freeze my tongue, I took my little dog named Grizzle and cut out for Salt River Bay to kill something for dinner. I got a good ways from home afore I knowed where I was, and as I had sweated some before I left the house my hat froze fast to my head, and I like to have put my neck out of joint in trying to pull it off. When I sneezed the icicles crackled all up and down the inside of my nose, like when you walk over a bog in winter time. The varmints was so scarce that I couldn't find one, and so when I come to an old log hut that had belonged to some squatter that had been reformed out by the nabors, I stood my rifle up agin one of the door posts and went in. I kindled up a little fire and told Grizzle I was going to take a nap. I piled up a heap of chestnut burrs for a pillow and straitened myself out on the ground, for I can curl closer than a rattlesnake and lay straiter than a log. I laid with the back of my head agin the hearth, and my eyes looking up-chimney so that I could see when it was noon by the sun, for Mrs. Crockett was always rantankerous when I staid out over the time. I got to sleep before Grizzle had done warming the eend of his nose, but I had swallowed so much cold wind that it laid hard on my stomach, and as I laid gulping and belching the wind went out of me and roared up the chimney like a young whirlwind.

So I had a pesky dream, and kinder thought, till I waked up, that I was floating down the Massassippy in a holler tree, and I hadn't room to stir my legs and arms, seein' that they were withed together with young saplings. While I was there and wan't able to help myself, a feller called Oak Wing that lived about twenty miles off, and that I had give a most almighty licking once, come and looked in with his blind eye that I had gouged out five years before. I saw him looking in one end of the hollow log, and he axed me if I wanted to get out. I told him to tie a rope to one of my legs and draw me out as soon as God would let him and as much sooner as he was a mind to.

But he said he wouldn't do it that way, he would ram me out with a pole. So he took a long pole and rammed it down agin my head as if he was ramming home the cartridge in a cannon. This didn't make me budge an inch, but it pounded my head down in between my shoulders till I look'd like a turtle with his head drawn in. This started my temper a trifle, and I ript and swore till the breath boiled out of the end of the log like the steam out of the funnel pipe of a steamboat.

Jest then I woke up, and seed my wife pulling my leg, for it was enermost sundown and she had come arter me. There was a long icicle hanging to her nose, and when she tried to kiss me, she run it right into my eye. I telled her my dream, and said I would have revenge on Oak Wing for pounding my head. She said it was all a dream and that Oak was not to blame; but I had a very diffrent idee of the matter.

So I went and talked to him, and telled him what he had done to me in a dream, and it was settled that he should make me an apology in his next dream, and that would make us square. For I don't like to be run upon when I'm asleep, any more than I do when I'm awake.

Drinking Up the Gulf of Mexico

You see, I told you in my last year's speech that I go in for Texas and Annexation, clar up to the very gravel stone, in spite o' all the Mixy Mexican Spanish brown an' red niggars, an' the Malgamation party in Uncle Sam's lands, who go in for Annexation with the blackies. I've heard all the four mile speeches, an' ten mile petitions on the subject, and I have come to the clar conclusion that the only thing that raley prevents the annexation, is the leetle deep-bellied pond called a Gulf, between Uncle Sam an' Texas; it stands like the Gulf between the rich man and Lazarus in the big book. It struck me like a thunderbolt, that if we war only to take that ar deep alligator water out o' the way, it would put an end to all no-gociation legislation, an' all that sort o' national nonsense, for then

157

little Texas an the States would annex themselves jist as nat'ral as two pumpkin vines, or as a gal o' seventeen annexes herself to a walkin' sprout o' lightnin, without the advice an' consent o' the old folks.

So, in order to remove this one little liquid obstacle out o' the way o' sich a great national wedding, I've jist straddled across the neck o' this pond, like Captain Collossus straddling the Roads, an' commenced drinking it up instanter. You see, when I open my flesh tunnel, it must come like a walkin' water spout, swaller arter swaller, till the bottom walks up as bare as a pumpkin.

Then, if any human crittur, Yankee, Texian or Mexican, dares to oppose instanter annexation, saw me up if I don't swallow them too. And arter that I'll jist mount my alligator, travel into the middle o' Mexico, lick all the tarnal Royalists out o' thar tarnal mustaches, strip Santa Anna of his power-ship, show him all naked in his villany and wodden-legged ambition; teach the natives, red niggers and creoles the true bred Yankee Independence and Republicanism; and then run for President myself!

Then if the critturs can't get along arter that, why I'll drink every spoonful of water between Texas and the United States, and annex her myself, in spite o' old Spain an' all the monkeys called monarchs in creation.

The Tame Bear

The creturs of the forest is of different kinds, like humans. Some is stupid and some is easy to larn. The most know-ing cretur that ever I seed war a barr that my darter Pinette picked up in the woods. It used to follow her to church, and at last it got so tame, it would come into the house, and set down in one corner of the fire-place to warm itself. I larned it to smoke a pipe and while it sot in one corner smoking, I sot in the other with my pipe. We couldn't talk to one another; but we would look, and I knowed by the shine of his eye what

he wanted to say, though he didn't speak a word. The cretur would set up o' nights when I war out late, and open the door for me. But it war the greatest in churning butter; it did all that business for the family. At last it got so civilized that it caught the hooping cough and died. My wife went to the minister and tried to get him to give the barr a christian burial; but the skunk war so bigoted that he wouldn't do it, and I told him the barr war a better christian than he ever war.

The Colonel Treeing a Ghost

I reckon as how you've all heard on ghosts, the tarnal flour-faced grave-desarters. I've seen every species o' these noble-blooded critters, and it takes me to tree 'em out about as slick as the lightnin trees a sharpened rod o' steel. The varmints is as feerd o' me as they are of a streak of daylight, bekase they know that I'm a little bit o' the supernatral myself; an' when I take my midnight walk o' recreation through a grave yard, I can hear the bone-boxes rattle as if thar war a hull ressurrection coming — if they don't then take my teeth for feet-stones. But some people are superstitious enough to believe in brute ghosts — well, that, you know, is equal to double yelked nonsense, for brutes are clar blood and bones, and can't have a spirit in 'em no how. But, howsever, the hull of our neighborhood once got into a sweaten terrification about the ghost of an old he-bar that I killed and mashed to death by a single hug, and they all swore they seed the ghost o' that identical bruin standin' upright in the place war I hugged the wind out o' him, drest in my cornshirt.

"Floods an airthquakes," thinks I, "perhaps my hug has squeezed the critter into petrefaction. If so I'll go and cut a few axe and razor hones off on him."

So one night a hull lot o' fellers took some bottle courage and led the way a piece, thinkin' to skeer my conscience by this bar's apparition. They hadn't got within ten paces o' the spot afore they all bellered out "Thar he is colonel, thar he is," and put off as if they'd fell on a camp o' red skull-cutters. I run up an' did see something looked tarnal like a bar's skull in a shirt.

"So," says I, "here's for another death hug"; an' I jist walked directly up to it, got on one knee, and grinned a little lightnin to see by, an' if the hull thing war anything more than a barked tree with two big knot holes in it, then take my eyes for green grog bottles.

Crockett's Account of the Concert in Kansas

One of our extremely sentimental and musical ladies of New York, who had long run mad after the Italian opera, with its foreign airs and foreign hairs, took a notion to emigrate with some of her agricultural relatives to Kansas, merely for the romance of the thing, and for some new sort of excitement. Like the fashionable belle who married an Indian, she put up with many privations and annoyances for the sake of the romance. She could get along without a street promenade, a fashionable gossip and scandal: "But," said she, "I shall positively expire from want of music and the dear opera. I am dying for the sounds and dulcet swells of a concert."

"A consart!" cried Crockett, who happened to hear her; "a consart, Miss! Do you mean for to come for to go for to think that we've not consarts an' operas in Kansas, Ma'am? Jist you walk along with me tonight, an' you shall hear both, by as hairy a set of vocalists as any Italian Opera House can show."

The lady was in raptures, and as soon as the night came on she was in perfect readiness, when Crockett lifted her into his opera-cab (a farm-cart), and drove out to the neighboring forest, which was alive with all kinds of wild beasts and hideous birds of night. At first, a screech-owl opened the programme with a direful scream —"Oh! what's that?" shrieked the trembling listener.

"That," said Crockett; "oh, that's only Signorina Screech-Owl-ine." Next came forth the horrid howl of a hungry wolf, which was soon joined by the growls of a grizzly bear. "There, Ma'am," said Crockett, "you hear the two great Bassos, Signors Wolfini and Bearini." Next thing, a panther put in his most shrill and horrid scream. "That, Ma'am," said Davy, "is the great tenora, Signor Painterini." In a few moments more, the whole and entire natural menagerie all broke out together — wolves, bears, wild hogs, wild horses, panthers, owls, and Indians, in a mingled roar which made the whole forest tremble

161

with the echo. At the same time, a huge bear walked out upon a fallen tree, with an Indian papoose in his paws. "Thar, Ma'am," shouted Crockett, "thar's the chorus an' fine-alley; ain't it fine. An' thar's Signor Bearini come out for a bucket of flowers."

The lady screamed, and fell into convulsions, and Crockett drove her home from the symphony.

AIDS PERSONAL AND BIBLIOGRAPHICAL

A WORD ON THE ALMANACS

NOTES TO FRONTIER HUMOR AND
LEGEND

AIDS PERSONAL AND BIBLIOGRAPHICAL

Interest in and knowledge of early American humor must be ascribed to a noteworthy series of studies and collections that has appeared since 1930.

In 1930 Franklin J. Meine, long a collector of the elusive newspapers, magazines and cheap books that held the written humor of the Old Southwest between 1830 and 1860, published *Tall Tales of the Southwest* as a volume in the Americana Deserta series under the general editorship of Bernard DeVoto. This anthology of many of the best of the humorous newspaper sketches (and not, as the title suggests, of collected oral tales) draws from the now established sources of the literature, Longstreet's *Georgia Scenes*, G. W. Harris's *Sut Lovingood*, Baldwin's *Flush Times*, and the volumes that found their way into the Peterson "Library of Humorous American Works." Introduction and selections are an excellent open sesame to a remarkable literature.

In 1931 Constance Rourke's *American Humor* superbly unraveled the deeper implications of the pagan comedy of the frontier, its creation of the national self-caricatures of the Yankee and the backwoodsman, its effulgence into a national folk expression, its indelible imprint in the higher literary achievements of American writers.

The one writer who carried the conventions of Southern humor to the point of literary artistry was Mark Twain. Bernard DeVoto in *Mark Twain's America*, published in 1932, explicitly and incisively illustrated the background and the tradition.

Two dominating myth-men straddled the Southwestern frontier. In 1933 Meine and Walter Blair assembled the legends of *Mike Fink: King of Mississippi Keel-Boatmen* from dusty and forgotten sources; in 1934 Miss Rourke drew in *Davy Crockett* a sober portrait from history that yet gave glimpses of legend's bizarre distortion.

The process of making available neglected materials was

continued in two rich collections of indigenous humor appearing in 1936 and 1937. Arthur Palmer Hudson ferreted out *Humor of the Old Deep South* from dark, remote and hidden corners, in all sorts of miscellaneous publications; travel books and journals, diaries and memoirs, newspapers and almanacs, miscellanies and galaxies, biographies and local histories yielded up the comic spirit that swept infectiously through Alabama, Mississippi and Louisiana in the decades before the Civil War. A broader canvas was spread by Walter Blair in portraying *Native American Humor (1800-1900)*; the sequence of nineteenth century rustic humor is traced from its beginnings with the Yankee comedians and Southern journalists through the professional funny men and local color humorists to its flowering in the writings of Mark Twain. This solid critical anthology rounds out the cycle of illuminating investigation begun by Mr. Meine.*

From the foregoing list of books† it can be seen that four scholars have been largely responsible for present knowledge of the colorful though neglected field of American folk humor; the contributions of Meine, Blair, DeVoto and Rourke have

*Of these seven books, all but Meine's and DeVoto's include scattered stories from the almanacs, the most interesting being "A Morning Hunt," reprinted by Miss Rourke in *American Humor*, and "Col. Crockett Beat at a Shooting Match," reprinted by Blair and Meine in *Mike Fink*. First use of the Crockett stories in an anthology of native humor goes back to Haliburton's *Traits of American Humor*, 1854, which lifted three without identifying their source. Scholarly notice of the almanacs was taken in 1925 in Clarence Brigham's bulletin "An Account of American Almanacs and Their Value for Historical Study," published in the Proceedings of the American Antiquarian Society for that year. The potentialities of the almanacs as a source of comic legend were first described by Miss Rourke in 1931 in her distinguished study of American humor. Interest in the ingenious woodcuts of the almanacs is shown by the reproduction of four of them in William Murrell's *A History of American Graphic Humor* (N. Y., 1933), and in their sporting yarns and descriptions of wild life by a full page facsimile of the covers of the Nashvilles for 1839, 1840, 1841, in the Grolier publication *Early American Sport*, compiled by Robert W. Henderson (N. Y., 1937).

†Attention is also called to the following monographs:

BLAIR, WALTER, "Inquisitive Yankee Descendants in Arkansas," American Speech, XIV, 11-22 (Feb., 1939).

CHITTICK, V. L. O., "Ring-tailed Roarers," The Frontier, XIII, 257-263 (May, 1933).

made American literary historians deeply their debtors. Mr. DeVoto and Mr. Meine have been personally most kind, and acquaintance with them has been not the least of the pleasures of this work. Most helpful direct source of information about the Crockett almanacs is the bibliographical discussion and check list of the almanacs in Miss Rourke's *Davy Crockett* (see pp. 247-258), compiled largely from the collection in the American Antiquarian Society at Worcester. This reference led me to the Society where through the kindness of Mr. R. W. G. Vail, the librarian, their splendid file of almanacs was placed at my disposal.

A debt of a more intangible nature must here be recorded. The present writer is only one of many who fumbles for adequate acknowledgment of the encouraging sympathy and the indefinable force of stimulus that make great teachers — Howard M. Jones, Francis O. Matthiessen, Perry Miller.

For a critical reading of portions of the introductory matter I am especially grateful to Professor Matthiessen, Mr. Meine, and John Bovey.

A WORD ON THE ALMANACS

Many questions of fact in connection with the Crockett almanacs remain to be answered. It has not been the purpose of this volume to attempt to deal with these questions. That purpose has been confined to making available to readers the better stories and woodcuts in the series. I have chosen not to include a list of the specific almanacs to which the stories here reprinted

DeVOTO, BERNARD, "The Matrix of Mark Twain's Humor," The Bookman, 172-178 (Oct., 1931).

EASTMAN, MAX, "The American Blend of Humor," in *Enjoyment of Laughter*, N. Y. 1936, Part VI, Ch. III, pp. 163-179.

JORDAN, PHILIP D., "Humor of the Backwoods, 1820-1840," Mississippi Valley Historical Review, XXV, 25-38 (June, 1938).

SHEPHARD, ESTHER, "The Tall Tale in American Literature," Pacific Review, II, 402-414 (Dec., 1921).

THOMPSON, W. F., "Frontier Tall Talk," American Speech, IX, 187-199 (Oct., 1934).

knife out, and my rifle had dropped down. He put up won of his hind claws agin my side, and I seed it war cuming to the *scratch* amazing sudden. So I called to my dog, and he cum up pretty slow till he seed what war the matter, and then he jumped a rod rite towards the bear. The bear got a notion that the dog was unfriendly to him. before he felt his teeth in his throat, and when Rough begun to gnaw his windpipe, the varmint ment there should be no love lost. But the bear had no notion of loosening his grip on me. He shoved his teeth so near my nose that I tried to cock it up out of his way, and then he drew his tongue across my throat to mark out the place where he should put in his teeth. All this showed that he had no regard for my feelings. He shook off the dog three or four times, like nothing at all, and once he trod on his head; but Rough stood up to his lick log and bit at him, but the varmint's hairs set his teeth on edge. All this passed in quicker time than a blind hoss can run agin a post, when he can't see whar to find it. The varmint made a lounge and caught hold of my rite ear, and so I made a grab at his ear too, and caught it between my teeth. So we held on to each others' ears, till

my teeth met through his ear. Then I tripped him down with one leg, and the cretur's back fell acrost a log, and I war on top of him. He lay so oncomfortable that he rolled off the log, and loosened his grip so much that I had a chance to get hold of my nife, and Rough dove into him at the same time. Seeing thar war two of us, he thought he would use one paw for each one. The varmint cocked one eye at me as much as to ax me stay whar I war till he could let go of me with one paw, and finish the dog. No man can say I am of a contrary disposition, though it come so handy for me to feel the haft of my big butcher, as soon as my rite hand war at liberty, that I pulled it out. The way it went into the bowels of the varmint war nothing to nobody. It astonished him most mightily. He looked as if he thought it war a mean caper, and he turned pale. If he didn't die in short time arterwards, then the Methodist parson eat him alive, that's all. When I cum to strip, arter the affair war over, the hairs of the bear's claws war up and down on my hide to such a rate that I might have been hung out for an American flag. The stripes showed most beautiful.

A Sailor's Yarn.

I always put grate dependence in my frend Ben Harding, and he never telled me any tuff yarn that warn't true; for I have seen as big wunders in the forrest, as he ever seed on the water. So put that to that, as the cat said when she stuck her tung into the kreem pot, and it proves 'em both true. Ben's last yarn war sumthing like this :—

I had a shipmate by the name of Bill Bunker. Bill was a queer chap, and was up to as many moves as a minnit watch that strikes every second. He want content to get threw the world with a reg'lar breeze and a moderate sea; but war always for having sum shine or another. He wood sooner climb over a coach than turn out for it; and whenever he fell down, he wood make bleeve he war drunk jist to raze a row with the watchmen.

Bill went won seeling voige in a little skooner called the Blackbird. I never telled you, Kurnill, how they knock them fellers over the nose; but that's neither here nor thar—Bill's scrape war on an Heand. Arter they had got pretty neer full of skins and sea-mammouth ile—sum calls 'em sea-illifants, but I spose when I tork to a Kongressman I must use high-floun lingo—they then steered away for home. They expected to make the land the nixt morning; but they seed nothing but an Heand. It war an outlandish place enuff, so full of scraggy trees and rocks that it looked as if you cood not find room to set down without scratching your fundaments to pieces. The Cappen concluded to lay under the ileand a few days, and so they cum to ankur. While they layed there they tarred down the rigging, painted the black streek on the vessel's side, korked the decks, and mended sales. But they didn't go ashore, as the Cappen had seen sum awful looking Ingens that war so ondecent as to wear very few close. Bill sed he wood be sworn thar warn't a tailor in the ileand that knowed how to make a pare of christian breeches.

So it war won fine sunny day when they war intending to be off the nixt morning, and they had the sales loosed to dry, when Bill, all at once, axed the Cappen to let him go ashore and have a kruice. This war a poser for the Cappen, as Bill was the only able seeman he had aboard, and he felt sartin that if he went ashore, he wood lose the number of his mess; for he wood hav his frolic out, and wood dance a jig if he war hanging on a gallus. He cood dance on a coffin or play kards on a tomb-stone. Bill woodn't take no for an ansur, and so the Cappen let him hav the boat. He skulled her ashore, and then walked into the intereur of the ileand. He found it looked better, as he went on. Thar war a plenty of green grass, and good water, and the birds war so thick, he wood hav thort he had been in the woods, if their wings had only been branches, instead of feathers. But he coodn't find no grog-shop, and so the water war almost as good as none, for every body knows that water without sumthing strong in it, is like a hansum bird that don't no how to sing.

Howsumever, when he got tired of walking about and seeing nobody, he worked down towards the shore; and now he determined to leave his cunnishawls on a big rok, befour he went aboard. So he got an old korking iron out of the bote, and begun to kut the fust letters of his name. Whilst he war at work, he seed out of won korner of his i, that thar war a little critter behind a tree—and then he watched slyly till he got a glimpse of its eyes. So he flung down his things and run thar. It war a Ingin gal, and Bill swears she war hansum. She tried to run, but Bill got up to her so quick she coodn't. Then she sunk back agin a tree, with her eyes on the ground, and looked as bashful as a monkey with his back broke. That struck Bill all aback, and he coodn't make up his mind rightly how he shood hail her, but he ranged up along side, and war going to mince up his mouth to speak her fair, when he sum how stuck the end of his queu into her eye. He didn't do it a proppus, but she jumped back, and thort he war going to board her in the smoke. He begun to make his pully-gees, and axed her pardon, and all that, but she woodn't trust him for a good while. She chattered away in her own lingo, and every once in a while she wood ketch hold of his queu and give it a twitch, and I spose she war sneering about it in her own language.

At last she got kinder kooled down, and then she let him take hold of her hand, while she led him to the place whar she lived—though she kept a lookout for the queu all the time, as she war afrade it wood be playing its tricks with her agin. She took him to a hut whar war about twenty savagers, and they all got up and run towards them making as big a noise as if the imps of the infurnul reguns had jist got a half holiday on a Saturday arternoon. Bill soon found out that this war the king's dawter, and while she telled 'em about the queu, they listened with their eyes and mouth wide open. As soon as she had done, they seized on Bill and tied him, hand and foot. Then they brot out a log of wood, and a ax that war made of flint, and sharp as need be. Bill begun to be skared; and then they took and laid him down with his hed on the log, and won grum looking feller cut up the ax. Bill thort his time war cum. His neck felt querer enuff. So he hurried and sed a short prayer and whistled won or two sam tunes for the good of his sole. Then the big savager lifted the ax over his hed, and down it cum—not on Bill's neck but on the queu, which it took off smack smooth close to his hed. The gal caught it up, and as soon as Bill war loosed, he didn't stop to see what she did with it, but cut dirt for the bote and got safe aboard the skooner.

---

belong. Such a list will be mailed upon request to the publisher's office. What is desirable is a complete check list of the almanacs and their contents.

The material included in this volume has been selected with a twofold intention: first, to present the more striking aspects of the central legendary personality, the peculiar quality of humor, the blend of human and superhuman elements; second, to represent the more popular anecdotal themes of the almanacs by the chapter groupings. Limitations of space have prevented the inclusion of the realistic pioneer and Indian stories; Daniel Boone, Simon Kenton, Kit Carson and George Washington creep into the almanacs in adventurous frontier anecdotes. Most of the material of this nature, however, is not original.

These almanacs are excessively rare, bring mounting prices in the old book market, and can not be consulted in anything like a complete series save with the greatest difficulty. Furthermore, there is little reward for the enthusiast who does reach the private or institutional collection, for in their fragile, pristine forms the almanacs seem expressly designed to cause the reader the greatest possible discomfort.* Fine print, an almost complete disregard for punctuation and paragraphing, intentional misspelling intensified by careless printing, result in what at times verges on an unintelligible jumble. It must be remembered, too, that there is no sequence and little consistency in the almanacs. A given almanac may have all, a few or no stories dealing with Crockett. The point of view and the style change without apology, although certain attitudes dominate. The stories themselves vary from juiceless hunting yarns to inspired tales of extravagant fantasy. Some almanacs have proved more fruitful than others—notably the 1839 Nashville and the Turner & Fishers for 1841, 1845 and 1848—but it can safely be said that the series is in its entirety remarkably successful in sustaining the raw and rowdy spirit of Davy Crockett's frontier.

*The present text by no means purports to be a faithful transcript of the almanacs. Liberties taken in wrestling with the text—and a good many are necessary —have been designed to produce clarity rather than consistency. Needless cacography has been eliminated, but no attempt has been made to systematize the spelling; "bear," for instance, is spelt bare, bar, barr, bear, seemingly at whim.

NOTES TO FRONTIER HUMOR AND LEGEND

page xv, NOTE 1 *The Big Bear of Arkansas,* W. T. Porter, ed. (Phila., Carey & Hart, 1845), "Chunkey's Fight with the Panthers," p. 139.

page xvi, NOTE 2 Crockett Almanac for 1836 (N. Y., Elton), "Crockett Outdone."

NOTE 3 *The Life of David Crockett* (N. Y., A. L. Burt, n. d.), p. 288.

NOTE 4 Crockett Almanac for 1841 (N. Y., Turner & Fisher), "A Miracle."

page xvii, NOTE 5 *Polly Peablossom's Wedding,* T. A. Burke, ed. (Phila., A. Hart, 1851), "How Mike Hooter Came Very Near 'Wolloping' Arch Cooney," p. 147.

NOTE 6 *A Quarter Race in Kentucky,* W. T. Porter, ed. (Phila., T. B. Peterson & Bros., copyright 1854), "Kicking a Yankee," pp. 163-4.

NOTE 7 *Sut Lovingood,* G. W. Harris (N. Y., Dick & Fitzgerald, copyright 1867), "Parson John Bullen's Lizards," p. 51.

NOTE 8 Ibid, "Blown up with Soda," p. 76; "Eaves-dropping a Lodge of Free Masons," p. 117.

NOTE 9 *Pickings from the Picayune,* D. Corcoran (Phila., T. B. Peterson & Bros., copyright 1846), "The Victim of Ambition," pp. 145-6.

NOTE 10 Crockett Almanac for 1854 (N. Y., Cozans).

NOTE 11 *A Quarter Race in Kentucky,* "Dick Harlan's Tennessee Frolic," p. 90.

NOTE 12 *Sut Lovingood,* "Dad's Dog School," p. 278.

NOTE 13 Crockett Almanac for 1841, "The Flower of Gum Swamp."

NOTE 14 *Sut Lovingood,* "Taurus in Lynchburg Market," p. 131.

NOTE 15 *The Widow Rugby's Husband,* J. J. Hooper (Phila., A. Hart, 1851), "Dick M'Coy's Sketches of his Neighbors," p. 35.

NOTES

page xviii, NOTE 16 These words are taken from several sources, the one most used being *Fisher's River* (*North Carolina*) *Scenes and Characters,* H. E. Taliaferro (N. Y., Harper and Bros., 1859), "Oliver Stanley."

NOTE 17 *Pickings from the Picayune,* "Jack Burns the Buster," p. 112.

NOTE 18 *Georgia Scenes,* A. B. Longstreet (N. Y., Harper & Bros., 1851), "The Fight," p. 54.

NOTE 19 *Streaks of Squatter Life,* J. S. Robb (Phila., T. B. Peterson & Bros., copyright 1848), "Seth Tinder's First Courtship," p: 177.

page xix, NOTE 20 *The Widow Rugby's Husband,* "A Night at the Ugly Man's," pp. 43-4.

NOTE 21 Ibid, pp. 50-1.

page xx, NOTE 22 *Theatrical Management,* Sol Smith (N. Y., Harper & Bros., 1868), "A Consolate Widow," pp. 102-3.

NOTE 23 Crockett Almanac for 1841, "A Street Fight."

NOTE 24 *Fisher's River,* "Fighting," p. 198.

page xxi, NOTE 25 *Col. Thorpe's Scenes in Arkansaw,* W. T. Porter, ed. (Phila., T. B. Peterson & Bros., copyright 1858), "Somebody in my Bed," pp. 170-1.

NOTE 26 *Sut Lovingood,* "Mrs. Yardley's Quilting," p. 139.

NOTE 27 *A Quarter Race in Kentucky,* "A Day at Sol Slice's," p. 181.

NOTE 28 *Sut Lovingood,* "Blown up with Soda," p. 75.

NOTE 29 *The Big Bear of Arkansas,* "Billy Warrick's Courtship and Wedding," p. 94.

NOTE 30 *Sut Lovingood,* "Mrs. Yardley's Quilting," p. 142.

NOTE 31 Ibid, "Sicily Burns's Wedding," p. 88.

page xxiii, NOTE 32 *The Hive of the Bee-Hunter,* T. B. Thorpe (N. Y., Appleton, 1854), "The Big Bear of Arkansas," p. 79.

NOTE 33 See Rowland Robinson, *Danvis Folks* (Rutland, Vt., 1934), p. 191; The American Joe Miller (London, 1865), p. 207; S. E. Morison, *Builders of the Bay Colony* (Boston, 1930), p. 248.

page xxiii, NOTE 34 See *Fisher's River,* pp. 63-9; Vance Randolph, *Ozark Mountain Folks* (N. Y., 1930), pp. 160-1; Joseph Kirkland, *Zury* (Boston & N. Y., 1882), p. 380.

NOTE 35 See G. L. Kittredge, *The Old Farmer and His Almanac* (Boston, 1904), p. 240; Randolph, *Ozark Mountain Folks,* pp. 143-4; E. A. Collins, *Folk Tales of Missouri* (Boston, 1935), pp. 36-9; Guy B. Johnson, *John Henry* (Chapel Hill, N. C., 1929), p. 144; Esther Shephard, *Paul Bunyan* (Seattle, 1924), pp. 16-18. This story also crops up in Paul Green's symphonic drama, "Potter's Field" (Green, *Out of the South,* N. Y., 1939, pp. 316-7.)

page xxv, NOTE 36 From the engrossing and authoritative source of Pecos Bill lore, Edward O'Reilly's article, "The Saga of Pecos Bill," in the Century Magazine for October, 1923 (106: 827-33).

NOTE 37 From John Chapman's column, "Mainly About Manhattan," New York Daily "News," Feb. 10, 1939.

INTERNATIONAL FOLKLORE

An Arno Press Collection

Allies, Jabez. **On The Ancient British, Roman, and Saxon Antiquities and Folk-Lore of Worcestershire.** 1852

Blair, Walter and Franklin J. Meine, editors. **Half Horse Half Alligator.** 1956

Bompas, Cecil Henry, translator. **Folklore of the Santal Parganas.** 1909

Bourne, Henry. **Antiquitates Vulgares; Or, The Antiquities of the Common People.** 1725

Briggs, Katharine Mary. **The Anatomy of Puck.** 1959

Briggs, Katharine Mary. **Pale Hecate's Team.** 1962

Brown, Robert. **Semitic Influence in Hellenic Mythology.** 1898

Busk, Rachel Harriette. **The Folk-Songs of Italy.** 1887

Carey, George. **A Faraway Time and Place.** 1971

Christiansen, Reidar Th. **The Migratory Legends.** 1958

Clouston, William Alexander. **Flowers From a Persian Garden, and Other Papers.** 1890

Colcord, Joanna Carver. **Sea Language Comes Ashore.** 1945

Dorson, Richard Mercer, editor. **Davy Crockett.** 1939

Douglas, George Brisbane, editor. **Scottish Fairy and Folk Tales.** 1901

Gaidoz, Henri and Paul Sébillot. **Blason Populaire De La France.** 1884

Gardner, Emelyn Elizabeth. **Folklore From the Schoharie Hills, New York.** 1937

Gill, William Wyatt. **Myths and Songs From The South Pacific.** 1876

Gomme, George Laurence. **Folk-Lore Relics of Early Village Life.** 1883

Grimm, Jacob and Wilhelm. **Deutsche Sagen.** 1891

Gromme, Francis Hindes. **Gypsy Folk-Tales.** 1899

Hambruch, Paul. **Faraulip.** 1924

Ives, Edward Dawson. **Larry Gorman.** 1964

Jansen, William Hugh. **Abraham "Oregon" Smith.** 1977

Jenkins, John Geraint. **Studies in Folk Life.** 1969

Kingscote, Georgiana and Pandit Natêsá Sástrî, compilers. **Tales of the Sun.** 1890

Knowles, James Hinton. **Folk-Tales of Kashmir.** 1893

Lee, Hector Haight. **The Three Nephites.** 1949

MacDougall, James, compiler. **Folk Tales and Fairy Lore in Gaelic and English.** 1910

Mather, Increase. **Remarkable Providences Illustrative of the Earlier Days of American Colonisation.** 1856

McNair, John F.A. and Thomas Lambert Barlow. **Oral Tradition From the Indus.** 1908

McPherson, Joseph McKenzie. **Primitive Beliefs in the North-East of Scotland.** 1929

Miller, Hugh. **Scenes and Legends of the North of Scotland.** 1869

Müller, Friedrich Max. **Comparative Mythology.** 1909

Palmer, Abram Smythe. **The Samson-Saga and Its Place in Comparative Religion.** 1913

Parker, Henry. **Village Folk-Tales of Ceylon.** Three volumes. 1910-1914

Parkinson, Thomas. **Yorkshire Legends and Traditions.** 1888

Perrault, Charles. **Popular Tales.** 1888

Rael, Juan B. **Cuentos Españoles de Colorado y Nuevo Méjico.** Two volumes. 1957

Ralston, William Ralston Shedden. **Russian Folk-Tales.** 1873

Rhys Davids, Thomas William, translator. **Buddhist Birth Stories; Or, Jātaka Tales.** 1880

Ricks, George Robinson. **Some Aspects of the Religious Music of the United States Negro.** 1977

Swynnerton, Charles. **Indian Nights' Entertainment, Or Folk-Tales From the Upper Indus.** 1892

Sydow, Carl Wilhelm von. **Selected Papers on Folklore.** 1948

Taliaferro, Harden E. **Fisher's River (North Carolina) Scenes and Characters.** 1859

Temple, Richard Carnac. **The Legends of the Panjâb.** Three volumes. 1884-1903

Tully, Marjorie F. and Juan B. Rael. **An Annotated Bibliography of Spanish Folklore in New Mexico and Southern Colorado.** 1950

Wratislaw, Albert Henry, translator. **Sixty Folk-Tales From Exclusively Slavonic Sources.** 1889

Yates, Norris W. **William T. Porter and the Spirit of the Times.** 1957